Pelican Books
What Freud *Really*

Dr Stafford-Clark is Physician-in-Charge of the
Department of Psychological Medicine and
Director of the York Clinic at Guy's Hospital, and
is also Consultant Physician of the Bethlem Royal
and Maudsley hospitals, and of the Institute of
Psychiatry of the University of London. During
the war he served in the Royal Air Force, became
a medical parachutist, and was twice mentioned in
dispatches.

In addition to his books and numerous professional
papers and articles he has also published poetry,
and has undertaken pioneer work in closed-circuit
colour and black-and-white television for psychiatric
teaching and demonstration in his own and other
hospitals. He designed and directed a number of
programmes in this field in public television,
including the B.B.C. 'Lifeline' and 'Brain and
Behaviour' series, and the 'Mind and Motive'
series for B.B.C. 2, as well as a special
programme commemorating the twentieth
anniversary of Freud's death, for the Independent
Television Authority. He was medical consultant
to John Huston's film, *Freud*. Since then he has
written and acted as technical director to three
award winning half-hour documentaries, 'And
Then There Was One', 'Time Out of Mind', and
'The Savage Voyage'. Each one of these films has
won gold medal acclamation in Britain and the
U.S.A.

David Stafford-Clark

What Freud *Really* Said

 Penguin Books

Penguin Books Ltd, Harmondsworth,
Middlesex, England
Penguin Books Inc., 7110 Ambassador Road,
Baltimore, Maryland 21207, U.S.A.
Penguin Books Australia Ltd, Ringwood,
Victoria, Australia

First published by Macdonald in the series
What They Really Said,
edited by A. N. Gilkes
Published in Pelican Books 1967
Reprinted 1969, 1971, 1973

Made and printed in Great Britain by
Richard Clay (The Chaucer Press) Ltd,
Bungay, Suffolk
Set in Monotype Imprint

For D. H., F. L., B. R. and D. S. C.
without whom it could not have been done.

Contents

SIGMUND FREUD

Born in Freiburg (now in Czechoslovakia), 1856
Went to Paris, 1885
Published *Studies on Hysteria: Preliminary Communication*
(with Breuer), 1886
Lived in Vienna, 1860–1938
Died in England, 1939

Preface

I hope the title of this book will make it clear that it is not an attempt to paraphrase or condense the material, either of Dalbiez' deservedly famous exposition and critique of psychoanalytical method and doctrine; or of the classical and definitive biography of Sigmund Freud by Ernest Jones. Indeed, it makes no attempt at biography whatsoever, and in so far as it explains and discusses its subject matter, the explanations and discussion are the sole and final responsibility of the author.

It is written for undergraduates and students of every and any kind who may be interested enough to read it. Other readers are of course welcome; but I would ask them to remember that when an author writes for the intelligent and inquiring young, he hopes always that the effect will be to stimulate and lure them to further thought and reading: never to stifle or lull them into abandoning their matchless quest.

D. S-C.

Acknowledgements

The author and publisher wish to thank the following for permission to quote from copyright material. Every endeavour has been made to trace the copyright holders of all such material included in this book but if any have inadvertently been omitted the publishers hereby express their regrets.

George Allen and Unwin Limited for permission to quote from *Freud: A Critical Re-Evaluation of His Theories* by Reuben Fine; and *The Interpretation of Dreams* and *Introductory Lectures on Psychoanalysis* both by Sigmund Freud; Ernest Benn Limited for permission to quote from *The Psychopathology of Everyday Life* by Sigmund Freud; The Bodley Head Limited for permission to quote from *The Wild Goose Chase* by Rex Warner; Dodd, Mead & Company for permission to quote from *Morbid Fears and Compulsions* by H. W. Frink; Paul Hamlyn Limited for permission to quote from *The Larousse Encyclopaedia of Mythology*; The Hogarth Press for permission to quote from *The Origins of Psychoanalysis* by Sigmund Freud, edited by Marie Bonaparte, Anna Freud and Ernst Kris, authorized translation by Eric Mosbacher and James Strachey; The Hogarth Press and The Institute of Psychoanalysis for permission to quote from *Psychoanalysis and Faith: The Letters of Sigmund Freud and Oskar Pfister*, edited by Heinrich Mengs and Ernst L. Freud, translated by Eric Mosbacher; also *The Standard Edition of the Complete Psychological Works of Sigmund Freud* translated into English under the General Editorship of James Strachey in collaboration with Anna Freud; The Author's Estate, International Authors and William Collins Sons & Company for permission to quote from *The Once and Future King* by T. H. White;

Longmans, Green & Company Limited for permission to quote from *Psychoanalytical Method and the Doctrine of Freud* by Roland Dalbiez; A. D. Peters & Company and William Collins Sons & Company for permission to quote from *The Autobiography of Charles Darwin* edited by Nora Barlow; Routledge & Kegan Paul Limited for permission to quote from *Totem and Taboo* and *Leonardo* both by Sigmund Freud.

Prelude

Merlyn, the magician and prophet of hindsight and foresight, speaks:

'Psychoanalyse her,' he said eventually, beginning to spin.

'But, Merlyn, wait! How are we to do this thing?'

'The usual method.'

'But what is it?' they cried in despair.

He disappeared completely, his voice remaining in the air.

'Just find out what her dreams are, and so on. Explain the facts of life. But not too much of Freud.'

T. H. White
The Once and Future King. 1958. *Collins*
(Fontana Books edition, p. 302)

Freud speaks:

Let us imagine, for instance, that in your leisure hours you take up a German, English or American novel. . . . After a few pages you come upon a first comment on psycho-analysis, and soon afterwards upon others, even though the context does not seem to call for them. You must not imagine that it is a question of applying depth-psychology to a better understanding of the characters in the book or of their actions – though, incidentally, there are other and more serious works in which an attempt of that kind is in fact made. No, these are for the most part facetious remarks intended by the author to display his wide reading and

intellectual superiority. Nor will you always form an impression that he really knows what he is talking about. . . .
New Introductory Lectures on Psychoanalysis. 1932–1936

S.E. Vol. XXII, p. 136

and earlier still, in private correspondence –

Why was it that none of the pious ever discovered Psychoanalysis? Why did it have to wait for a completely Godless Jew?

Sigmund Freud, 1928

The three items set out as a prelude to this short book consist in effect of a statement by an author, followed by a protest, and then by a cry of anguish, from someone who had good reason to feel threatened by that statement. This is an historical situation; but what makes it an appropriate beginning to this book is that, in every essential point, history has been reversed by the presentation of these items. Such actual history as will find its place here will show that characteristically, throughout the whole of Sigmund Freud's life and work, it was *his* destiny to make statements based on work which he had done, which aroused both protests and cries of anguish from other people; usually from people who wanted nothing of the help which Freud gave and was prepared to teach others to give, but believed that they and their society had much to lose from an acknowledgement of the truth which Freud sought to proclaim.

The reversal of history is also chronological. Not only do the items selected put an otherwise unchallenged author in the position of the one uttering the statement, and Freud in the position of the recipient uttering the protest: but also, reference to the dates will show that in fact the cry of anguish came first, the protest later, and the particular example of the provocation by which both these can be seen to be justified, some twenty-five years later still. Re-reading those three items in this context, we are reminded of the Red Queen in *Alice Through the Looking Glass* who screamed before she hurt herself, knowing that the hurt would come and that a scream would be drawn from her.

When Freud uttered the statements quoted from his *New Introductory Lectures on Psychoanalysis* and from his earlier letter, he had already good reason to know that the greater part of his work would never find universal understanding, still less acceptance, during his lifetime. He was a wide and enthusiastic reader. He might have taken comfort from some well-known lines by Rudyard Kipling, which indeed could have seemed to have been written precisely to describe his own experience:

> If you can bear to hear the truth you've spoken,
> Twisted by knaves, to make a trap for fools . . .[1]

For, even after over fifty years have passed since the first of his major communications was made, this distortion of one of the most significant pieces of human thought and discovery in the history of ideas still continues. The author of *The Once and Future King* is only one of innumerable educated people who have led less educated people to believe that, whatever the merits or demerits of psychoanalysis, it can be separated from what Freud really said, and might indeed be more acceptable if it were. Conversely, it is still possible for people to gain the impression that they know what Freud really said without ever having read a word that he himself wrote.

It is the limited purpose of this short communication to re-dress the balance of distortion and misunderstanding for people whose minds remain sufficiently open, and whose interest is sufficiently unbiased, to want to know what kind of contribu-tion a single man made to human understanding. This was a man whose name will always rank with those of Darwin, Coper-nicus, Newton, Marx and Einstein; someone who really made a difference to the way the rest of us can begin to think about the meaning of human life and society. The thoughts of such men, the way that their minds worked, and the ways in which they sought to convey the outcome of this work in what they said and wrote, are part of the heritage of the human race. Their statements do not have to be accepted as dogma, above or beyond critical reflection or consideration. But we owe it to ourselves, no less than to them, to pay attention to what they really said.

Psychoanalysis was and will always be Freud's original creation. Its discovery, exploration, investigation and constant revision formed his life's work. It is manifest injustice, as well as
wantonly insulting, to commend psychoanalysis, still less to invoke it '. . . without too much of Freud'. And yet the author of
The Once and Future King is only one of many who have committed this light-hearted outrage without even so much as re-
cognizing the nature of their act. No one person in fact is to be
blamed for it. Freud himself recognized this, in these words:

You may raise the question of why these people – both the ones
who write books and the conversationalists – behave so badly;
and you may incline to the view that the responsibility for this
lies not only on them but also on psychoanalysis. I think so too.
What you come upon as prejudice in literature and society is an
after-effect of an earlier judgement – the judgement, namely, that
was formed upon the young psychoanalysis by the representa-
tives of official science. I once complained of this in an historical
account I wrote, and I shall not do so again – perhaps that once
was too often – but it is a fact that there was no violation of
logic, and no violation of propriety and good taste, to which the
scientific opponents of psychoanalysis did not give way at that
time.* The situation recalled what was actually put in practice

* Opposition to Freud's theories began from the moment he first
attempted to convey them to his colleagues. Ernest Jones, in his
classical biography, *Sigmund Freud – His Life and Work*, devotes an
entire chapter in the second volume to this opposition. Freud himself
referred to it in *An Autobiographical Study* and in his essay on the
history of the psychoanalytic movement. Instances selected at various
stages of Freud's career will provide our examples here.

The first followed Freud's return from working with Charcot in
Paris. Freud had described some cases of hysteria which he had
studied in men. The President of the Viennese Society of Medicine
declared that this was incredible, and Dr Meynert, a leading neurologist of the time, challenged Freud in a friendly but incredulous fashion
to discover a single case of hysteria in men in Vienna. Freud records
that he tried to produce several such cases to the Society, but the
senior physicians in whose departments he discovered them refused to
allow him either to observe the patients or to work with them. The

in the Middle Ages when an evil-doer, or even a mere political
opponent, was put in the pillory and given over to maltreatment
by the mob. You may not realize clearly, perhaps, how far upwards in our society mob-characteristics extend, and what mis-
conduct people will be guilty of when they feel themselves part
of a crowd and relieved of personal responsibility. At the beginning of that time I was more or less alone and I soon saw that
there was no future in polemics, but that it was equally senseless
to lament and to invoke the help of kindlier spirits, for there
were not courts to which such appeals could be made. So I took

––––––––––

basis of their refusal was epitomized by one old surgeon, who protested: 'But, my dear sir, how can you talk such nonsense? Hysteria
means the uterus. So how can a man be hysterical?' This statement
was made at a time when the brain as the organ of mind was fully
accepted by contemporary physicians.

In his history of the psychoanalytic movement, Freud recalls:

'I innocently addressed a meeting of the Vienna Society of Psychiatry and Neurology with Krafft-Ebing in the chair . . . expecting
that the material losses I had willingly undergone would be made up
for by the interest and recognition of my colleagues. I treated my
discoveries as ordinary contributions to science and hoped they
would be received in the same spirit. But the silence which my
communications met with, the void which formed itself about me,
the hints that were conveyed to me, gradually made me realize that
assertions on the part played by sexuality in the aetiology of the
neuroses cannot count upon meeting with the same kind of treatment as other communications. I understood that from now onwards I was one of those who have "disturbed the sleep of the
world", as Hebbel says, and that I could not reckon upon objectivity
and tolerance.'[2]

At a congress of German neurologists and psychiatrists in Hamburg
in 1910, Professor Wilhelm Weygandt interrupted a discussion in
which Freud's theories had been mentioned, by banging his fist on the
table and shouting: 'This is not a topic for discussion at a scientific
meeting: it is a matter for the police.' In the same year Professor
Oppenheim, a leading German neurologist, and author of an established textbook on the subject, demanded that Freud's writings should
be subject to a boycott in any respectable psychiatric institution.

another road. I made a first application of psychoanalysis by explaining to myself that this behaviour of the crowd was a manifestation of the same resistance which I had to struggle against in individual patients. I refrained from polemics myself and influenced my adherents, when little by little they appeared, in the same direction. This procedure was the right one. The interdict which lay upon psychoanalysis in those days has been lifted since then. But, just as an abandoned faith survives as a superstition, just as a theory which has been given up by science continues to exist as a popular belief, so the original outlawing of psychoanalysis by scientific circles persists today in the

---

There was an immediate response from the audience, where all the directors of psychiatric establishments present leapt to their feet to declare their innocence of any connexion with such heresies.

In his own autobiography Freud records that one of his opponents boasted of silencing his patients if they dared to mention anything sexual, and concluded from this that such a technique satisfied the doctor concerned that he had a right to judge the part played by sexuality in the aetiology of the neuroses. In 1911 a patient came to the Berlin Psychiatric Clinic complaining of an obsessional impulse to lift women's skirts in the streets. The director of the clinic said to his students: 'This is an opportunity to test the supposed sexual nature of such obsessions. I will ask the patient if this applies to old women as well as young, in which case it obviously can't be erotic.' The patient replied: 'Yes, to all women, even to my mother and sister. . . .' The director triumphantly ordered the entry in the case notes to describe the case as definitely not sexual.

A story which Freud first recounted in 1914, in his *History of the Psychoanalytic Movement*, is repeated in his autobiographical study. It concerns a colleague who had attended one of Freud's lectures, and afterwards remarked that he had already written a book against Freud's theories but had never read what Freud had published about them. He had been told by the director of his own unit that such research was unnecessary and 'not worth while'. Referring to this briefly in 1925, eleven years later, Freud adds sadly:

'The man in question, who has since become a professor, has gone so far as to repudiate my report of the conversation and to throw doubts in general upon the accuracy of my recollection. I can only say that I stand by every word of the account I then gave.'[3]

facetious contempt of the laymen who write books or make conversation. So this will no longer surprise you.[4]

New Introductory Lectures on Psychoanalysis, 1932.

It had long ceased to surprise Freud. Nevertheless he continued, up to the time of his death, to expound his work to the uninitiated although otherwise educated lay public, as well as to the professional audiences who had reason to know something of the revolution in thought for which he had been responsible. Indeed, what he conveyed without rebuke or indignation displayed not simply his indomitable faith in the value of human communication but also his deep conviction that whatever of truth underlay his ideas would always ultimately find its reflection in the experience of his readers.

The foundation of this conviction was that, while what he had to say was new, the material upon which his observations were made and his theories were built was as old and as universal as the inmost experience of the human race. Freud was a genius: but the confusing and often seemingly contradictory tangle of human experience which confronted him was no different from that which confronted and still confronts every practising doctor and, indeed, every student of man. It was his destiny to seek the truth from within this tangle, with patient humility, and to proclaim his findings with tenacious courage.

Before we examine these in detail, it will be helpful to have the outline of his work before us, in the general order in which he himself discovered and collected it. The essential starting point began with Freud's confrontation, as a practising physician, with the timeless, tremendous, and perplexing challenge of hysteria, both in the form of hysterical symptoms and in that disorder of character which has come to be called the hysterical personality; phenomena which have always lain like a drawn sword across the path of medical progress.

For centuries this challenge had been answered by dismissing it as unreal, so that sufferers from hysterical symptoms were simply excluded from the arena of medical care; or by expelling or displacing this challenge to other areas of human concern. In the Middle Ages, the preoccupation of various sects of Christendom with demonology and the persecution of heretics had enabled patients with hysterical symptoms or personalities to be included among those charged with witchcraft, and thereby excluded from the concern of medicine, to be tortured or burnt to death instead. The close of this era had left the problem of hysteria unsolved, to stumble falteringly back upon the clinical scene, where it remained as unwelcome as it had always been.

With remarkable vision, Freud perceived that hysteria is in fact 'a real sickness'; that hysterical symptoms are genuinely experienced by patients. Hysterical pain hurts as much, hysterical anaesthesia numbs as much, hysterical amnesia forgets as much, as any other way in which pain, numbness, or forgetfulness can be experienced by human beings. Once he had recognized this, Freud had to find room in his own understanding for the commonplace but baffling paradox that these suffering, numbed, or amnesic patients had no structural basis in their nervous system for the disabilities which afflicted them.

Freud went to Paris to learn more from one of the greatest contemporary neurologists, Professor Charcot. Charcot was at that time demonstrating that hysterical symptoms could be reproduced in their entirety in patients who had been hypnotized, and under hypnosis had been told, with the authority of the hypnotist, that such symptoms existed in their minds and bodies and could not be denied. Such patients were indistinguishable from others suffering from hysteria, in that they too felt pain or lost sensation entirely, shook and trembled or became completely paralysed, lost their memory or later performed actions for which they could not account, but which were in fact the result of commands given them during the hypnotic state.

For Charcot, these phenomena were interesting experimentally but did not have any particular therapeutic significance. Moreover, he believed that the capacity to undergo hypnosis, together with the capacity to develop hysterical symptoms, were evidence of degeneration, probably due to some structural inadequacy of the nervous system, and therefore conveniently removed those so equipped or afflicted from the responsibility of further medical care. They were subjects for demonstration; but to Charcot all that they ultimately demonstrated was that the symptoms underlying their unconscious mental activity were a sign of irreversible disability, a disorder capable of clinical demonstration but not of lasting relief.

It is one of the signs of genius that its possessor asks questions which have simply never occurred to other people in the face of the same situation. Freud asked himself whether these powerful unconscious mental mechanisms, which alone could explain the phenomena of hysteria and hypnosis, might well exist in all human beings, and play an important role in their lives, of which they themselves could not normally be fully aware. This was the beginning of his discovery of psychoanalysis, but even this tentative theory was received with the utmost hostility by Freud's neurological colleagues in Vienna, when he returned there from Paris. Nevertheless, one man had used hypnosis to allay hysteria, and with this man Freud set up a collaboration to which he was always most generously to acknowledge a profound indebtedness.

The colleague was Breuer, a physician practising in fashionable Vienna, and the first publication heralding the development of psychoanalysis was a joint work produced by Breuer and Freud, and entitled *Studies on Hysteria*.

Perhaps the most important single discovery recorded in this work is that the precipitant factor in hysteria can as readily be psychological as physical. Yet, when it was psychological, it was characteristically never remembered by the patient, or even available to the patient's memory by introspection. Freud saw that the banishment of such significant and emotionally charged memories from consciousness required an active mechanism operating at an unconscious level, as well as the relegation of such emotionally charged material to what would have to be an unconscious area of mental life. This led him to the concept of repression: the dynamic, compulsive, but completely unconscious forgetting of unbearable, threatening or disturbing experiences. He had yet to recognize that the existence of this repression in everybody, including himself, was to provoke not only unconscious resistance to ultimate recovery in patients suffering from hysteria, but also a comparable resistance, on the part of practically everyone, to the very nature of the discoveries which he and Breuer were making through their work with such patients. New ideas tend always to excite resistance, but these excited violent hostility and irrational denial; moreover, not only they, but their originators, became socially unacceptable.

Even when Freud had begun to recognize this, and to accept it as part of the inevitable price to be paid for publishing the results of his work, he had still to discover in himself the nature of his own unconsciously repressed emotions and experiences, and their impact upon his own life and judgement.

Why should there be this resistance? Reviewing his own and Breuer's shared clinical experience, Freud was able to discover a consistent theme underlying each one of their cases. This theme was a sexual one. Repressed sexuality, the unconscious denial of a forbidden and now forgotten sexual wish or experience, seemed to him to be a fundamental cause of the great majority of neuroses which he had encountered.

Resistance to this possibility took its first toll in Breuer's ultimate and anguished repudiation of the implications of his work with Freud. Breuer had suffered the embarrassment of discovering that one of his women patients had developed an overwhelming sexual attachment to him. He had felt able to

respond only by breaking off that patient's treatment. Ultimately, such attachment proved in fact to be the emergence of
precisely that repressed sexual feeling which Breuer and
Freud's own discoveries had already implied must be expected
to complicate treatment of this kind. Breuer reacted to this
critical discovery by rejecting the unbearable implications of the
knowledge on which it was based; even though this knowledge
was derived from his own and Freud's shared experience. He
was in fact endorsing by his feelings exactly that theory which
he was then ready to deny. Finally he felt compelled to deny
even the knowledge itself. Freud had to go on alone.

In his further and now single-handed exploration of this
material, Freud began to discover buried sexual memories in
all his patients. These memories frequently took the form of
recollections of sexual seduction in infancy by the parent of the
opposite sex. At first Freud accepted these memories as his-
torically accurate, even though they pointed to the possibility
of large-scale seduction of infant daughters by their fathers. It
was some time before he discovered that in the majority of
cases these memories were what he came to call 'screen
memories': memories which corresponded not to events which
had actually taken place but to phantasies of what in fact had
never happened. They represented what the patient had
feared or wished might happen, which had been at first consciously denied, and then unconsciously repressed to emerge
in the course of analysis with a vividness and apparent
reality indistinguishable in the patient's mind from other
childhood memories which were capable of historical verifica-
tion.

These infantile sexual phantasies fulfilled wishes or recalled
fears which were also bound up with what Freud's patients had
come to believe he sought to discover from them, and which
therefore, once discovered in this way, would relieve them of
their present symptoms.

This remarkable recognition of the existence of screen

memories going back to infantile phantasies led to a further
brilliant revelation on the part of Freud himself. This was the
concept of infantile sexuality – the innocent, unformed, but
excruciating passion of the child for the parent. Once again,
this theory was greeted by an outburst of derision and protest.
As Freud himself said, whatever might be the reception
accorded to this theory, it was based on observation of infantile behaviour which any attentive mother or nursemaid had
always been able to see for herself, but which every adult later
felt bound in conspiracy to reject or deny.

When these earliest views were first published, Freud found
himself involved in such hostility, dissension and calumny that
this opposition temporarily threatened his work to the point
where, for a time, he was tempted to abandon it.

But the existence of an active, dynamic, unconscious area of
mental life, one of whose vital mechanisms was the process of
compulsive involuntary forgetting of overwhelmingly disturbing and emotionally charged wishes or memories, against whose
re-emergence tremendous resistance could be discovered in
every human being – all these phenomena were by now too
evident to Freud to be disregarded, and moreover far too
important in the understanding and treatment of nervous
disorders for him to be able to turn his back on them. In retrospect, the road he had travelled could be seen to be an
inescapable one for a physician determined to penetrate to
the root of hysterical symptoms, and possessed of the courage,
intelligence and tenacity to do so.

Hypnosis, which had previously been used simply to reinforce denial of symptoms and their origin by suppressing them,
had led him first with the help of Breuer to catharsis, whereby
hitherto unknown memories and their emotions flooded consciousness and thereafter reversed the pattern of the symptoms,
to recovery. But no sooner had this pattern seemed to have so
profound and fundamental an element of sexual emotion, than
Breuer had denied it. Writing of this, Freud said:

When I later began more and more resolutely to put forward the significance of sexuality in the aetiology of neuroses, he [Breuer] was the first to show the reaction of distaste and repudiation which was later to become so familiar to me, but which at that time I had not yet learnt to recognize as my inevitable fate.[5]

Because of the element of suggestion always inseparable from it, and mindful particularly of the effect of that element in possibly forcing screen memories upon susceptible patients, Freud soon found reasons for abandoning hypnosis altogether. At different times he selected different reasons as having been crucial. But some time after he had ceased to attempt to hypnotize his patients he finally abandoned even any kind of physical contact with them, preferring to sit out of their range of vision behind them, simply demanding of them that they say out loud, and without conscious reservation or criticism of any kind, everything that came into their minds, as one association followed another. This process, to which Freud gave the name 'free association', was the final step in the foundation of a technique of analysis between doctor and patient. It provided the means whereby everything which he was subsequently to discover could emerge. What follows will be an account, necessarily concise, of the fruits of that knowledge, of the theories which Freud developed from it, of their impact upon his own further thought, and of the final structure of psychoanalytic knowledge, theory and technique, both for research and treatment, which he gave to medicine, and indeed to mankind.

Freud did not set out with the intention of being a practising doctor, still less a psychotherapist. When he was a child he had enjoyed imagining himself as a great general or statesman: Hannibal was a favourite hero of his. Later in his life science attracted him as the surest road to true power and understanding for the man of integrity, and medicine seemed to combine the opportunity for application of scientific knowledge with the pursuit of individual interest. However, Freud only finally entered the practice of clinical medicine for financial reasons, partly because the research work at which he had shown great promise did not seem to be leading him anywhere in terms of promotion, and partly because, like very many other young men of his and every other day, he was in love, he wanted to get married and he needed more money than he was earning.

Breuer helped Freud, not only with encouragement and advice but with money. They also shared each other's experience, and Breuer passed some of his patients on to Freud, until both of them were working largely with hysterical cases, and decided to pool and publish their findings. This was the historical beginning of psychoanalysis, and it is interesting to see what Freud said in their first and only joint publication. This personal digression occurred in the course of his discussion of some of the cases which he had presented in the book:

I have not always been a psychotherapist. Like other neuropathologists, I was trained to employ local diagnoses and electroprognosis, and it still strikes me myself as strange that the case histories I write should read like short stories and that, as one might say, they lack the serious stamp of science. I must console myself with the reflection that the nature of the subject is evidently responsible for this, rather than any preference of my own. The fact is that local diagnosis and electrical reactions lead nowhere in the study of hysteria, whereas a detailed description of mental processes such as we are accustomed to find in the works of imaginative writers enables me, with the use of a few psychological formulas, to obtain at least some kind of insight into the course of that affection. Case histories of this kind are intended to be judged like psychiatric ones; they have, however, one advantage over the latter, namely an intimate connection between the story of the patient's sufferings and the symptoms of his illness – a connection for which we still search in vain in the biographies of other psychoses. . . .[6]

The two authors recounted how they had discovered that any experience capable of calling up distressing feelings – such as those of fright, anxiety, shame or physical pain – could operate as the starting-point of hysterical symptoms. Whether in fact such a starting-point actually led on to the development of hysterical illness depended,

naturally enough, upon the susceptibility of the person affected (as well as on another condition which will be mentioned later). In the case of common hysteria it not infrequently happens that, instead of a single major trauma, we found a number of partial traumas forming a group of provoking causes. . . .[7]

The Greek word *trauma*, literally meaning a wound, was consistently used for the provocative stress in hysterical illness at that time. The authors continued:

But the causal relation between the determining psychical trauma and the hysterical phenomenon is not of a kind implying that the trauma merely acts like an *agent provocateur* in releasing the symptom, which thereafter leads an independent existence. We must presume rather that the psychical trauma – or more precisely the memory of the trauma – acts like a foreign body which long after its entry must continue to be regarded as an agent that is still at work; and we find the evidence for this in a highly remarkable phenomenon which at the same time lends an important practical interest to our findings.

For we found, to our great surprise at first, that *each individual hysterical symptom immediately and permanently disappeared when we had succeeded in bringing clearly to light the memory of the event by which it was provoked and in arousing its accompanying affect, and when the patient had described that event in the greatest possible detail and had put the affect into words.* Recollection without affect almost invariably produces no result. . . .[8]

The word 'affect' here is used in the accepted psychiatric sense of emotion.

They went on to conclude that not only were these provocative stresses essentially causal despite the fact that they were not present in consciousness; but also that the determining process whereby they were produced, their affects, continued to operate in some way or another indefinitely in time – 'not indirectly, through a chain of intermediate causal links, but as the *directly* releasing cause'.[9]

They then stated:

Hysterics suffer mainly from reminiscences.

The release of emotion connected with these causes was called 'abreaction', and really what was happening in the cases described by Breuer and Freud was that an abreaction of long-buried, significant emotional material was being induced through the release of some barrier which existed in normal consciousness, but which was dissolved at least temporarily in hypnosis. Drawing further upon this, and upon the general implications of their observations, they wrote:

'Abreaction', however, is not the only method of dealing with the situation that is open to a normal person who has experienced a psychical trauma. A memory of such a trauma, even if it has not been abreacted, enters the great complex of associations, it comes alongside other experiences, which may contradict it, and is subjected to rectification by other ideas. After an accident, for instance, the memory of the danger and the [mitigated] repetition of the fright becomes associated with the memory of what happened afterwards – rescue and the consciousness of present safety. Again, a person's memory of a humiliation is corrected by his putting the facts right, by considering his own worth, etc. In this way a normal person is able to bring about the disappearance of the accompanying affect through the process of association.

To this we must add the general effacement of impressions, the fading of memories which we name 'forgetting' and which wears away those ideas in particular that are no longer affectively operative. Our observations have shown, on the other hand, that the memories which have become the determinants of hysterical phenomena persist for a long time with astonishing freshness and with the whole of their affective colouring. We must, however, mention another remarkable fact, which we shall later be able to turn to account, namely, that these memories, unlike other memories of their past lives, are not at the patients' disposal. On the contrary, *these experiences are completely absent from the patients' memory when they are in a normal psychical state, or are only present in a highly summary form*. Not until they have been questioned under hypnosis do these memories emerge with the undiminished vividness of a recent event.[10]

Still further and final general observations from these studies, which contained a great deal of detailed case material which need not be considered here, were embodied in two further memorable statements which once again will be quoted exactly as they were first written:

It may therefore be said that the ideas which have become pathological have persisted with such freshness and affective strength because they have been denied the normal wearing away processes by means of abreaction and reproduction in states of uninhibited association.[11]

In effect, what cannot be remembered cannot be left behind; an insight never before expressed in a scientific paper, although

Wordsworth indicates an intuitive awareness of it, by his reference to 'Thoughts that do often lie too deep for tears'.[12]
Shakespeare, too, over 350 years earlier, puts into the mouth of
Macbeth this urgent request addressed to the characteristically
helpless physician of that day:

> Canst thou not minister to a mind diseas'd;
> Pluck from the memory a rooted sorrow;
> Raze out the written troubles of the brain;
> And, with some sweet oblivious antidote,
> Cleanse the stuff'd bosom of that perilous stuff
> Which weighs upon the heart?[13]

'Yes,' said Freud and Breuer, 'you can do that.' A more
hopeful answer than the physician was able to give Macbeth,
but, as it turned out, an answer which unfortunately was every
bit as unacceptable to those who received it, because it substituted a threatening and seemingly dangerous insight for a
total incapacity. The authors summarized the key to their
thesis in these words:

*It will now be understood how it is that the psychotherapeutic
procedure which we have described in these pages has a curative
effect. It brings to an end the operative force of the idea which was
not abreacted in the first instance, by allowing its strangulated
affect to find a way out through speech; and it subjects it to associative correction by introducing it into normal consciousness (under
light hypnosis) or by removing it through the physician's suggestion,
as is done in somnambulism accompanied by amnesia.*[14]

The case histories themselves have to be read in detail to be
fully appreciated. But they demonstrate over and over again
the remarkable fidelity with which the pattern taken by the
emerging symptoms symbolizes both the nature of the pre-
cipitating trauma, and also the nature of the magical solution
of the conflict, produced by the trauma in the patient's
mind.

One of Freud's patients was experiencing severe attacks of

facial neuralgia, which he had already treated by conventional methods, without success, on a number of occasions. Freud describes his interest in discovering whether this too could turn out to have a psychological basis.

Using hypnosis he called up the traumatic scene in the patient's buried experience, whereupon she saw herself back in a period of great exasperation towards her husband. She described the conversation which she had had with him, and a remark of his which she had felt as a bitter insult. Suddenly she put her hand to her cheek, gave a loud cry of pain, and said, 'It was like a slap in the face.' With this her pain and her attack were both at an end. But this was not the end of the neuralgia. Other occasions had to be recalled and ultimately Freud had to take his patient back to her first attack of neuralgia more than 15 years before she had consulted him. Here there was no symbolization but what he described as:

a conversion through simultaneity. She saw a painful sight which was accompanied by feelings of self-reproach, and this led her to force back another set of thoughts. Thus it was a case of conflict and defence. The generation of the neuralgia at that moment was only explicable on the assumption that she was suffering at the time from slight toothache or pains in the face, and this was not improbable, since she was just then in the early months of her first pregnancy.

Thus the explanation turned out to be that this neuralgia had come to be indicative of a particular psychical excitation by the usual method of conversion. . . .[15]

Freud himself was clearly aware that the necessity to assume neuralgia as coincidental at the time of the original trauma weakened the case for the type of purely psychological origin which most of his clinical evidence seemed to suggest. He went on to give examples which seemed to him to prove that physical suffering could occur through symbolization alone.

One of the most striking was that of a girl of fifteen, who, while lying in bed under the watchful eye of her strict grandmother, suddenly cried out with pain. She had dreamed she had felt a penetrating pain in her forehead, between her eyes, which then lasted for weeks. This pain recurred intermittently during the next thirty years, and during analysis of the symptom, she was able to remember and tell Freud that at the time her grandmother had given her a look 'so piercing' that she felt it had gone right into her brain. She had in fact been afraid that the old woman was viewing her with suspicion. At the moment of removing this recollection she was able to laugh, and the pain disappeared.

Despite the comparative success of their joint publication, Breuer and Freud never collaborated in any further published material. The original communication was reprinted, but the attention it received was not entirely favourable. Between the publication of the preliminary work by Breuer and Freud, in 1893, and the subsequent publication of the case histories and the authors' theoretical formulations, Freud himself had produced one single communication with the title *The Neuropsychoses of Defence*.

This in fact heralded not only the break with Breuer but the beginning of the independent emergence of Freud's own concept of psychoanalysis. The basic difference of opinion between the two authors, upon which Freud was later to lay considerable emphasis, concerned the part played by sexual impulses in the causation of hysteria. But even here the expressed difference was at the time less clear than one could have expected. Freud's belief in the sexual origin of hysteria emerged in his chapter on the psychotherapy of hysteria, with which the studies conclude. This was specifically his own contribution, just as the previous section had been Breuer's. Even so, he did not state there, as he was later to insist so emphatically, that the sexual aetiology would invariably be found in all cases of hysteria. In Breuer's own section he too had laid emphasis on the important part played by sexuality in neurosis, writing, for instance, that:

sexual instinct is undoubtedly the most powerful source of persisting increases of excitation (and consequently of neuroses).[16]

and finally declaring:

The great majority of severe neuroses in women have their origin in the marriage bed.[17]

Nevertheless, as is pointed out by the editor of the *Collected Works*, when commenting on this already latent conflict between the two men, Freud had privately regarded Breuer as a man full of doubts and reservation, always insecure in his own conclusions. An extreme instance of this occurred in a letter of 8 November 1895, to Dr Fliess, by now Freud's principal confidant. This letter was written about six months after the publication of the *Studies on Hysteria*. Freud writes:

Not long ago Breuer made a big speech about me at the Doktorenkollegium, in which he announced his conversion to belief in the sexual aetiology [of the neuroses]. When I took him on one side to thank him for it, he destroyed my pleasure by saying: 'All the same I don't believe it.' Can you understand that? I can't.[18]

The editor comments that something of the kind can be read between the lines of Breuer's own contribution to the studies, wherein we have the picture of a man half afraid of his own remarkable discoveries. It was inevitable, remarked the editor, that Breuer should have been even more disconcerted by the premonition of still more unsettling discoveries yet to come; it was equally inevitable that Freud in turn should feel hampered and irritated by his co-author's uneasy hesitations.

In his individual contribution to the theory of hysteria and its treatment, Freud had already gone far beyond what Breuer was ultimately able to accept. He set it down uncompromisingly, but not without deference to the senior author.

Thus starting out from Breuer's method, I found myself engaged in a consideration of the aetiology and mechanism of the neuroses in general. I was fortunate enough to arrive at some serviceable findings in a relatively short time. In the first place I was obliged to recognize that, in so far as one can speak of determining causes which lead to the *acquisition* of neuroses, their aetiology is to be looked for in *sexual* factors.[19]

There was nothing new in this for Freud. In the only other paper he had published on psychological matters, *The Neuropsychoses of Defence*, he had already outlined ways in which he believed the defence of the conscious personality, and its peace of mind, against disturbing or forbidden sexual excitement, might produce symptoms. They might be converted into other and quite separate phenomena as in hysteria; or they might remain in consciousness, but be robbed of the emotion which accompanied them, which would then attach to other and apparently meaningless acts or thoughts – the theory of the false connexion which was later to become extremely important in Freud's approach to obsessive compulsive disorders – or, finally, they might be completely banished from normal consciousness at the price of disrupting it so much that the patient was in a psychotic state: either completely unaware of and unable to deal with his actual surroundings on a realistic basis, or deprived of all normal memory of his identity and predicament.

The important thing about this paper was not simply the interesting and extremely ingenious hypotheses which it expressed, which were all based upon Freud's actual clinical work with patients, and the symptoms which they displayed. Equally important is the fact that Freud here gave expression to his own deepening conviction that sexuality lay at the root of all neurosis, and that the extent to which disturbance of sexual feelings could produce psychological symptoms of any kind was related to the amount of nervous energy involved.

He was later to propose a classification of neuroses in which some were termed actual neuroses, being disturbances of psychological equilibrium and well-being *directly and physically related to the frustration or the excessive discharge of sexual energy*; while all the rest were psychoneuroses, in which an unconscious mechanism converted the disturbance of sexual function into complicated, indirect, but nevertheless highly disruptive and symbolic symptoms. Before the completion of his contribution to *Studies on Hysteria* Freud had already indicated the inevitability of the break not only with Breuer but with hypnosis, and even with catharsis.

It would be unfair if I were to try to lay too much of the responsibility for this development upon my honoured friend Dr Josef Breuer. For this reason the considerations which follow stand principally under my own name.
   When I attempted to apply to a comparatively large number of patients Breuer's method of treating hysterical symptoms by an investigation and abreaction of them under hypnosis, I came up against two difficulties, in the course of dealing with which I was led to an alteration both in my technique and in my view of the facts. (1) I found that not everyone could be hypnotized who exhibited undoubted hysterical symptoms and who, it was highly probable, was governed by the same psychical mechanism. (2) I was forced to take up a position on the question of what, after all, essentially characterizes hysteria and what distinguishes it from other neuroses.[20]

At this point it becomes necessary to stand back from our close examination of the beginnings of Freud's contribution to psychology, and from his first tentative, but rapidly developing, explorations in some of the words he actually used, the better to grasp the meaning and significance of the concept of psychoanalysis as it first took shape in its author's mind. By now Freud had decided that the clue to understanding neuroses in general, and hysterical symptoms in particular, was to look beneath the surface of the patient's symptoms and to seek the unconscious factor in their production. He had recognized clearly that the patient could not know this unconscious factor himself, but nevertheless that no one other than the patient could lead Freud to the discovery of what it was, and therefore to the possibility of relief of the symptoms.

Significantly, not only was the key factor unconscious, it seemed destined to remain unconscious unless and until a successful and penetrating search brought it to light. This search would have to take account of the fact that the process by which the material had become unconscious was in no way accidental, but was in fact a defence mechanism whereby over-whelmingly emotionally charged material was consigned to the secret files: an area of mental life beyond the direct reach of memory or introspection.

His own experience with patients had convinced him that he knew the essential nature of this highly charged experience, and that in every case it must ultimately be sexual. He had still not reached the point at which he could be sure that this sexual origin occurred at the earliest point in life; that is, during the first few years. However, he had recognized that resistance to the emergence of this material took the form both of the patient's inability further to cooperate in treatment and, sometimes, of outright hostility to the doctor presenting it.

The opposite emotion could also be expected; namely, an investment of love, which might have a frankly sexual nature, for the doctor who was conducting the treatment: love which would prove to have roots deeper in the past than the patient could possibly know, and would precede, often by very many years, both the symptoms of the illness and the doctor's appearance on the scene in an attempt to relieve it.

Freud himself said that the concepts of unconscious mental activity, repression, resistance and transference were the fundamental pillars of psychoanalysis. Transference was the name he gave to the investment of powerful and previously buried emotion in the physician undertaking treatment. Moreover, he coined the name 'psychoanalysis' to describe the process, once he had become certain that the mere liberation of charged material, without either interpretation or recognition on the patient's part of its particular significance in his life and its relationship to his symptoms, was not alone sufficient.

By the time psychoanalysis as a process had been given a name, Freud had already given up hypnosis altogether, but was still sitting beside his patient and, usually, placing his hand on the patient's forehead to reinforce his powerful exhortations that the patient could and must trace associations and uncover links between buried thoughts and repressed memories. After a time Freud realized that even this procedure had grave disadvantages, in that it retained at least an element of suggestion and, in some instances, brought into the transference an element of actual erotic stimulation. This aspect of his discovery proved to have extremely far-reaching effects in psychoanalysis, so that even to this day many analysts will not examine their patients physically, but will refer them to a colleague, in no way related to the psychoanalytic procedure, for such examination.

We have seen already that the consideration of what Freud really said inevitably involves us also in an examination of what he did. In this, as in any other application of theory to experimental use, technique is vitally important. There is bound to be a certain amount of overlap between these two areas, but only by seeing both in historical perspective can we build up a picture of how his ideas developed and how, finally, he was in a position to formulate what could be called the general theory of psychoanalysis, together with its technique and applications; and so come to reap the harvest of knowledge to which he has provided access, and which must be further considered in a later stage of this book. At the moment we are exactly where Freud was, at the point of our own examination of his work: we have seen emerging certain new and remarkable ideas, but we have yet to discover what their total impact will be, and how they will fit into an over-all and comprehensive theory of mental life. Where did Freud go from here?

We are not now concerned with what happened before Freud had left the laboratory and entered the consulting room. There he practised at first as a neurologist and examined his patients as any other doctor would have done at that stage in the history of medicine, using his hands, eyes, ears and nose, and such simple instruments as light, lenses, vibrating tuning forks, specula, reflex hammers and a stethoscope. Many of his patients proved, on examination, to have no evidence of structural lesions: to be in this respect indistinguishable from normally healthy people. Patients of this kind were of no medical interest to their doctors and could expect neither forbearance nor even enduring courtesy. They were traditionally shown the door, either with the assurance that there was nothing wrong with them or else with the advice that all they needed to do was to pull themselves together; indeed, they might have been subjected to those gratuitous insults, still unfortunately not unknown in medicine, whereby patients complaining of distress are told not only that there is no basis for it, when all they know is that there must be, but also that they are wasting their own and the doctor's time in asking for help at all.

It was at this point that Freud turned to hypnosis and a variety of physical treatment at that time called electrotherapy,* both of which were conventional and traditional in the treatment of neurotic patients. Neurotic patients themselves were, in those days, simply that significant group of human beings who suffered from afflictions unrecognized by doctors: afflictions having their origin in disturbance of function rather than of structure.

Hypnosis has been known as long as medicine has been

* Electrotherapy in the late nineteenth century was simply a form of local electrical stimulation of skin and muscle areas. It bore no relation to the electrical treatment of the brain to be discovered some fifty years later.

practised. In using it, Freud was attempting to master a technique as mysterious as it was suspect. Its most recent cause of disrepute had originated in Vienna, and was still remembered with shame and chagrin. Some 100 years earlier an Austrian, Anton Mesmer, born at Weil, near Lake Constance, on 23 May 1733, after graduating in medicine in Vienna, had become influenced by astrology and the new discoveries of electricity and magnetism. He evolved therefrom his own theory and technique of treatment of nervous disorder, based on what he called 'animal magnetism'.

This was essentially the technique of hypnotism, practised with a great deal of additional paraphernalia and suggestion, in all of which Mesmer himself probably believed, although he has often been regarded as an enterprising, aggressive and quick-witted charlatan. His theories rested upon the assumption that the universe was filled with a magnetic fluid which permeated everything and conveyed the influence of the stars. Mesmer claimed to be able to manipulate the balance and effects of this fluid by personal power. He constructed an apparatus like a cauldron, from which projected iron rods. These, grasped by the patients, who could then hold each other's hands, brought them under the influence of Mesmer's magnetic wand which he waved about in conducting the treatment.

In 1784 the Academy of Sciences in France investigated Mesmer's activities and came to the conclusion that 'imagination with magnetism produces convulsions and that magnetism without imagination produces nothing'. This infuriated Mesmer, who was always keenly conscious of his own dignity and position, but although scepticism and ridicule were employed against him with a powerful effect his personal prestige remained, and the effects which he produced continued to receive careful study by individual physicians.

Furthermore, mesmerism fulfilled an unquestionable need of the times. It was in fact the only available treatment for neuroses, since the medical profession were little interested and had nothing to offer, and the priests and lawyers had withdrawn from the scene with the ending of the era of persecution. The work of Pinel, the Tukes, Benjamin Rush and others in America was still essentially dedicated to the demonstrably insane; but the proportion of the population afflicted with mental illness outside the new mental hospitals was probably not a great deal smaller than it is today, and sought, as it still seeks, relief wherever it might be found.

Mesmer had left Vienna for Paris towards the end of the eighteenth century, almost exactly 100 years before Freud began his own work with nervous patients. But Vienna was still very sensitive about the contumely and ridicule which Mesmer had brought upon Viennese medicine, not because he had failed, but because he had succeeded in many cases by what were demonstrably unscientific and unashamedly theatrical techniques. The reinstatement of hypnosis in medical practice, following its final severance from the whole mumbo-jumbo of animal magnetism, had owed much to practising physicians such as Liébeault and Bernheim in France, and James Braid, Elliottson, and a surgeon of the East India Company called Esdaile from England. Charcot's famous demonstrations at the Hôpital Saltpetriere in Paris rivalled Mesmer's in theatrical effect: but they were not aimed at treatment. Nevertheless, Charcot's reputation as a neurologist was at that time the greatest sanction for the re-employment of hypnosis in neurology.

The overtones of quackery which clung to hypnosis were remembered with particular sensitivity in Vienna. When Freud returned from Paris and began to claim that, by using hypnosis once again in a relatively unorthodox way, knowledge might be forthcoming about the minds of his patients as opposed to a purely authoritative dismissal of their symptoms, he was bound to encounter antipathy to his claims. Electrotherapy, despite an origin comparable to the speculations of

Mesmer about magnetism and astrology, was a much more respectable technique. But Freud had found it completely useless. Such apparent improvement as might follow it he considered to be due only to the effect of suggestion. His own observations on this score, which directly concern his abandonment both of hypnosis and of electrotherapy, are significant.

Anyone who wants to make a living from the treatment of nervous patients must clearly be able to do something to help them. My therapeutic arsenal contained only two weapons, electrotherapy and hypnotism; for prescribing a visit to a hydropathic establishment after a single consultation was an inadequate source of income. My knowledge of electrotherapy was derived from W. Erb's textbook (1882), which provided detailed instructions for the treatment of all the symptoms of nervous diseases. Unluckily I was soon driven to see that following these instructions was of no help whatever and that what I had taken for an epitome of exact observations was merely the construction of phantasy. The realization that the work of the greatest name in German neuropathology had no more relation to reality than some 'Egyptian' dream-book, such as is sold in cheap book shops, was painful, but it helped to rid me of another shred of the innocent faith in authority from which I was not yet free. So I put my electrical apparatus aside, even before Moebius had saved the situation by explaining that the successes of electric treatment in nervous disorders (in so far as there were any) were the effect of suggestion on the part of the physician.

With hypnotism the case was better. While I was still a student I had attended a public exhibition given by Hansen the 'magnetist', and had noticed that one of the subjects experimented upon had become deathly pale at the onset of cataleptic rigidity and had remained so as long as that condition lasted. This firmly convinced me of the genuineness of the phenomena of hypnosis. Scientific support was soon afterwards given to this view by Heidenhain; but that did not restrain the professors of psychiatry from declaring for a long time to come that hypnotism was not only fraudulent but dangerous and from regarding hypnotists with contempt. In Paris I had seen hypnotism used freely as a method for producing symptoms in patients and then removing them again. And now the news reached us that a school had arisen at Nancy which made an extensive and remarkably successful use of suggestion, with or without hypnosis, for therapeutic purposes. It thus came about, as a matter of course, that in the first years of my activity as a physician my principal instrument of work, apart from haphazard and unsystematic psychotherapeutic methods, was hypnotic suggestion.

This implied, of course, that I abandoned the treatment of organic nervous diseases; but that was of little importance. For on the one hand the prospects in the treatment of such disorders were in any case never promising, while, on the other hand, in the private practice of a physician working in a large town, the quantity of such patients was nothing compared to the crowds of neurotics, whose number seemed further multiplied by the way in which they hurried, with their troubles unsolved, from one physician to another. And, apart from this, there was something positively seductive in working with hypnotism. For the first time there was a sense of having overcome one's helplessness; and it was highly flattering to enjoy the reputation of being a miracle-worker. It was not until later that I was to discover the drawbacks of the procedure. At the moment there were only two points to complain of: first, that I could not succeed in hypnotizing every patient, and secondly, that I was unable to put individual patients into as deep a state of hypnosis as I should have wished. With the idea of perfecting my hypnotic technique, I made a journey to Nancy in the summer of 1889 and spent several weeks there. I witnessed the moving spectacle of old Liébeault working among the poor women and children of the labouring classes. I was a spectator of Bernheim's astonishing experiments upon his hospital patients, and I received the profoundest impression of the possibility that there could be powerful mental processes which nevertheless remained hidden from the consciousness of men. Thinking it would be instructive, I had persuaded one of my patients to follow me to Nancy. This patient was a very highly gifted hysteric, a woman of good birth, who had been handed over to me because no one knew what to do with her. By hypnotic influence I had made it possible for her to lead a tolerable existence and I was always able to take her out of the misery of her condition. But she always relapsed again after a short time, and in my ignorance I attributed this to the fact that her hypnosis had never reached the stage of somnambulism with amnesia. Bernheim now attempted several times to bring this about, but he too failed. He frankly admitted to me that his great therapeutic successes by means of suggestion were only achieved in his hospital practice and not with his private patients. . . .

I must supplement what I have just said by explaining that from the very first I made use of hypnosis in *another* manner, apart from hypnotic suggestion. I used it for questioning the patient upon the origin of his symptom, which in his waking state he could often describe only very imperfectly or not at all. Not only did this method seem more effective than mere suggestive commands or prohibitions but it also satisfied the curiosity of the physician, who, after all, had a right to learn something of the origin of the phenomenon which he was striving to remove by the monotonous procedure of suggestion.[21]

In all his writings Freud had very little to say about the actual technique of hypnosis which he used. This is indeed unimportant from the point of view of psychoanalysis, because hypnosis was abandoned completely before psychoanalysis had really begun. But the period of transition from catharsis and hypnosis to the final and formal procedure of analysis is an interesting one. During this time Freud used to sit behind his patients, and use a technique which he came to call the pressure technique.

With the patient lying upon the couch, Freud would lean forward and place his hand on the patient's forehead, or both his hands on either side of the patient's head, and tell the patient that whatever resistance was being encountered would be overcome by this pressure, so that the patient would then perceive the idea or memory which was eluding him. Freud used this technique to overcome blocks in the patient's verbal

associations to their own unconscious mental processes. At one
point in his writings he recorded that the method of pressure
seemed to work in every case, and could overcome every
difficulty. He had carried over into it one interesting remnant
of his first experience in treating patients by hypnosis, namely
that when an idea or memory seemed elusive, so that pressure
was needed to produce it, the outcome of that pressure might
quite readily be a picture in the patient's mind, rather than
anything else. Patients under hypnosis had thus frequently
visualized past scenes which they had previously forgotten,
and which were in fact vitally significant to the material under
examination.

But here again Freud ran into difficulties, sometimes because
no scene or recollection would come, sometimes because
patients tended to disparage what they maintained was the
obvious unimportance of such fragments as occurred to them.
With continued pressure Freud occasionally got what seemed
at first quite inexplicable responses. On one occasion one of his
patients, asked whether she had seen anything or had any recollection under the pressure of his hand, replied:

'Neither the one nor the other, but a word has suddenly oc-
curred to me.'
  'A single word?'
  'Yes, but it sounds too silly.'
  'Say it all the same.'
  '*Concierge.*'
  'Nothing else?'
  'No.'

I pressed a second time and once more an isolated word shot
through her mind:
  'Night-gown.'

I saw now that this was a new sort of method of answering,
and by pressing repeatedly I brought out what seemed to be a
meaningless series of words:
  '*Concierge*' – 'night-gown' – 'bed' – 'town' – 'farmcart.'
  'What does all this mean?' I asked.

She reflected for a moment and the following thought occurred to her:

' It must be the story that has just come into my head. When I was ten years old and my next elder sister was twelve, she went raving mad one night and had to be tied down and taken into the town on a farm-cart. I remember perfectly that it was the *concierge* who overpowered her and afterwards went with her to the asylum as well.'

We pursued this method of investigation and our oracle produced another series of words, which, though we were not able to interpret all of them, made it possible to continue this story and lead on from it to another one. Soon, moreover, the meaning of this reminiscence became clear. Her sister's illness had made such a deep impression on her because the two of them shared a secret; they slept in one room and on a particular night they had both been subjected to sexual assaults by a certain man. The mention of this sexual trauma in the patient's childhood revealed not only the origin of her first obsessions but also the trauma which subsequently produced the pathogenic effects.

The peculiarity of this case lay only in the emergence of isolated key-words which we had to work into sentences; for the appearance of disconnectedness and irrelevance which characterized the words emitted in this oracular fashion applies equally to the complete ideas and scenes which are normally produced under my pressure. When these are followed up, it invariably turns out that the apparently disconnected reminiscences are closely linked in thought and that they lead quite straight to the pathogenic factor we are looking for. For this reason I am glad to recall a case of analysis in which my confidence in the products of pressure was first put to a hard test but afterwards brilliantly justified.[22]

Even when a visual picture came readily, Freud learned that it was only the prelude to the importance of the verbal associations which followed it. He recorded that:

the patient gets rid of the picture by turning it into words.

In this way the final technique of free association began to emerge. But later in the treatise in which he described this, Freud returned to the problem of resistance and then for the first time came upon the concept of transference.

He records how he learned:

with astonishment . . . *that we are not in a position to force anything on the patient about the things of which he is ostensibly ignorant, or to influence the products of the analysis by arousing an expectation. . . .*

Another observation, which is constantly repeated, relates to the patient's spontaneous reproductions. It may be asserted that every single reminiscence which emerges during an analysis of this kind has significance. An intrusion of irrelevant mnemic images (which happen in some way or other to be associated with the important ones) in fact never occurs. An exception which does not contradict this rule may be postulated for memories which, unimportant in themselves, are nevertheless indispensable as a bridge, in the sense that the association between two important memories can only be made through them.[23]

The promise of this procedure, and the remarkable results that it achieved, led Freud to spend all his time in interviews of anything from twenty to fifty minutes with individual patients, fortnightly, weekly, or even several times a week, for as long as the patients would come and the problem remained to be solved. And although the patients were paying and Freud was working hard at this intensive but often monotonous and tediously repetitive analytic procedure, he was increasingly aware that, against every one of their apparent interests, patients would be overcome by resistances so that treatment would be held up, money would be spent for nothing, the illness would continue and Freud himself would be frustrated in his aims.

Writing of this towards the end of his chapter on the psychotherapy of hysteria, Freud said that where the pressure technique failed to elicit any reminiscence of any kind, in spite of every assurance and insistence, there seemed to him to be two possibilities:

. . . either, at the point at which we are investigating, there is really nothing more to be found – and this we can recognize from the complete calmness of the patient's facial expression; or we have come up against a resistance which can only be overcome later, we are faced by a new stratum into which we cannot yet penetrate – and this, once more, we can infer from the patient's facial expression, which is tense and gives evidence of mental effort. But there is yet a third possibility which bears witness equally to an obstacle, but an external obstacle, and not one inherent in the material. This happens when the patient's relation to the physician is disturbed, and it is the worst obstacle that we can come across. We can, however, reckon on meeting it in every comparatively serious analysis.

I have already indicated the important part played by the figure of the physician in creating motives to defeat the psychical force of resistance. In not a few cases, especially with women and where it is a question of elucidating erotic trains of thought, the patient's cooperation becomes a personal sacrifice, which must be compensated by some substitute for love. The trouble taken by the physician and his friendliness have to suffice for such a substitute. If, now, this relation of the patient to the physician is disturbed, her cooperativeness fails, too; when the physician tries to investigate the next pathological idea, the patient is held up by an intervening consciousness of the complaints against the physician that have been accumulating in her. In my experience this obstacle arises in three principal cases.

(1) If there is a personal estrangement – if, for instance, the patient feels she has been neglected, has been too little appreciated or has been insulted, or if she has heard unfavourable comments on the physician or the method of treatment. This is the least serious case. The obstacle can easily be overcome by discussion and explanation, even though the sensitiveness and suspiciousness of hysterical patients may occasionally attain surprising dimensions.

(2) If the patient is seized by a dread of becoming too much

accustomed to the physician personally, of losing her independence in relation to him, and even of perhaps becoming sexually dependent on him. This is a more important case, because its determinants are less individual. The cause of this obstacle lies in the special solicitude inherent in the treatment. The patient then has a new motive for resistance, which is manifested not only in relation to some particular reminiscence but at every attempt at treatment. It is quite common for the patient to complain of a headache when we start on the pressure procedure; for her new motive for resistance remains as a rule unconscious and is expressed by the production of a new hysterical symptom. The headache indicates her dislike of allowing herself to be influenced.

(3) If the patient is frightened at finding that she is transferring on to the figure of the physician the distressing ideas which arise from the content of the analysis. This is a frequent, and indeed in some analyses a regular, occurrence. Transference on to the physician takes place through a *false connection*.[24]

Freud went on to give an example of this last possibility in which, at the end of an analytic session, the patient suddenly experienced a desire to be kissed by him. This desire proved to be one which she had had many years earlier but had repressed, in connexion of course with an entirely different man. But at first she was unable either to recognize it or to proceed with the analysis because of the block which it imposed upon her train of thought.

In every case analysis of the transference itself paved the way to a final resolution of the difficulty. But as the analysis of the transference became more and more important, so anything which might reinforce the transference, and particularly any physical gesture or contact which might be interpreted even unconsciously by the patient as a physical caress, had to be abandoned. Ultimately Freud saw his patients regularly, never hypnotized, and rarely touched them, and scrutinized with particular care both his own and their demeanour even in such apparently trivial and social aspects of the consultation as the way in which they entered or left the room, closed or left him to close the door, or touched or failed to touch his hand on their departure. Technique and theory were beginning to become increasingly related to one another in terms of unconscious significance.

3 *The Interpretation of Dreams*

Working over the ideas that occur to patients when they submit to the main rule of psychoanalysis is not our only technical method of discovering the unconscious. The same purpose is served by two other procedures: the interpretation of patients' dreams and the exploitation of their faulty and haphazard actions. . . .

The interpretation of dreams is in fact the royal road to a knowledge of the unconscious; it is the securest foundation of psychoanalysis and the field in which every worker must acquire his convictions and seek his training. If I am asked how one can become a psychoanalyst, I reply: 'By studying one's own dreams.' Every opponent of psychoanalysis hitherto has, with a nice discrimination, either evaded any consideration of *The Interpretation of Dreams* or has sought to skirt over it with the most superficial objections. If, on the contrary, you can accept the solutions of the problems of dream-life, the novelties with which psychoanalysis confronts your minds will offer you no further difficulties.[25]

(*From the Third of Five Lectures on Psychoanalysis delivered in America and published in 1900*)

Nothing that Freud ever wrote better sets out the kernel of his views about the indispensable techniques of psychoanalysis and the lessons to be learned from them. The procedure of the analytic session, now lasting up to an hour and with free association as its single rule, together with the interpretation of the patient's dreams and the analysis of their faulty and haphazard actions, ultimately led Freud to every one of the principles which he was eventually to incorporate in the final structure of psychoanalysis as he defined it. In this and the succeeding chapter we shall consider the two techniques thus indicated, and what they taught Freud and enabled him to teach others.

Dreams had always had a particular fascination for Freud. It will be remembered that when he was searching for a metaphor to convey the misleading worthlessness of electrotherapy as prescribed by Professor Erb, he said that it was of no more value than an Egyptian dream book. He knew a great deal more about dream books, and the popular belief that dreams could foretell the future as well as reflect the present state of people's fortunes, than most of his educated colleagues in Vienna. It was not until he turned to the study of dreams himself, in an elaboration of his method of free association, that he was to discover the monumental breakthrough which this technique made possible.

We can return to Freud's own exposition, in the condensed form in which he gave it in his five American lectures, to see how he himself chose to introduce the subject of the interpretation of dreams to an interested but uninformed audience whom he hoped would follow it further by reading from his original work:

You should bear in mind that the dreams which we produce at night have, on the one hand, the greatest external similarity and internal kinship with the creations of insanity, and are, on the other hand, compatible with complete health in waking life. There is nothing paradoxical in the assertion that no one who regards these 'normal' illusions, delusions and character-changes with astonishment, instead of comprehension, has the slightest prospect of understanding the abnormal structures of pathological mental states otherwise than as a layman. You may comfortably count almost all psychiatrists among such laymen.

I invite you now to follow me on a brief excursion through the region of dream-problems. When we are awake we are in the habit of treating dreams with the same contempt with which patients regard the associations that are demanded of them by the psychoanalyst. We dismiss them, too, by forgetting them as a rule, quickly and completely. Our low opinion of them is based on the strange character even of those dreams that are not confused and meaningless, and on the obvious absurdity and nonsensicalness of other dreams. Our dismissal of them is related to the uninhibited shamelessness and immorality of the tendencies openly exhibited in some dreams. It is well known that the ancient world did not share this low opinion of dreams. . . .

In the first place, not all dreams are alien to the dreamer, incomprehensible and confused. If you inspect the dreams of very young children, from eighteen months upwards, you will find them perfectly simple and easy to explain. Small children always dream of the fulfilment of wishes that were aroused in them the day before but not satisfied. You will need no interpretative art in order to find this simple solution; all you need do is to enquire into the child's experiences on the previous day (the 'dream-day'). Certainly the most satisfactory solution of the riddle of dreams would be to find that adults' dreams too were like those of children – fulfilments of wishful impulses that had come to them on the dream-day. And such in fact is the case. The difficulties in the way of this solution can be overcome step by step if dreams are analyzed more closely.

The first and most serious objection is that the content of adults' dreams is as a rule unintelligible and could not look more unlike the fulfilment of a wish. And here is the answer. Such dreams have been subjected to distortion; the psychical process underlying them might originally have been expressed in words quite differently. You must distinguish the *manifest content of the dream*, as you vaguely recollect it in the morning and laboriously (and, as it seems, arbitrarily) clothe it in words, and the *latent dream-thoughts*, which you must suppose were present in the unconscious. This distortion in dreams is the same process that you have already come to know in investigating the formation of hysterical symptoms. It indicates, too, that the same interplay of mental forces is at work in the formation of dreams as in that of symptoms. The manifest content of the dream is the distorted substitute for the unconscious dream-thoughts and this distortion is the work of the ego's forces of defence – of resistances. In waking life these resistances altogether prevent the repressed wishes of the unconscious from entering consciousness; and during the lowered state of sleep they are at least strong enough to oblige them to adopt a veil of disguise. Thereafter, the dreamer can no more understand the meaning of his dreams than the hysteric can understand the connection and significance of his symptoms.

You can convince yourself that there are such things as latent dream-thoughts and that the relation between them and the manifest content of the dream is really as I have described it, if you carry out an analysis of dreams, the technique of which is the same as that of psychoanalysis. You entirely disregard the apparent connections between the elements in the manifest dream and collect the ideas that occur to you in connection with each separate element of the dream by free association according to the psychoanalytic rule of procedure. From this material you arrive at the latent dream-thoughts, just as you arrived at the patient's hidden complexes from his associations to his symptoms and memories. The latent dream-thoughts which have been reached in this way will at once show you how completely justified we have been in tracing back adults' dreams to children's dreams. The true meaning of the dream, which has now taken the place of its manifest content, is always clearly intelligible; it has its starting-point in experiences of the previous day, and proves to be a fulfilment of unsatisfied wishes. The manifest dream, which you know from your memory when you wake up, can therefore only be described as a *disguised* fulfilment of *repressed* wishes.

You can also obtain a view, by a kind of synthetic work, of the process which has brought about the distortion of the unconscious dream-thoughts into the manifest content of the dream. We call this process the 'dream-work'. It deserves our closest theoretical interest, since we are able to study in it, as nowhere else, what unsuspected psychical processes can occur in the unconscious, or rather, to put it more accurately, *between* two separate psychical systems like the conscious and unconscious. Among these freshly discovered psychical processes those of *condensation* and *displacement* are especially noticeable. The dream-work is a special case of the effects produced by two different mental groupings on each other – that is, of the consequences of mental splitting; and it seems identical in all essentials with the process of distortion which transforms the repressed complexes into symptoms where there is unsuccessful repression.

You will also learn with astonishment from the analysis of dreams (and most convincingly from that of your own) what an unsuspectedly great part is played in human development by impressions and experiences of early childhood. In dream-life the child that is in man pursues its existence, as it were, and retains all its characteristics and wishful impulses, even such as have become unserviceable in later life. There will be brought home to you with irresistible force the many developments, re-pressions, sublimations and reaction-formations, by means of which a child with a quite other innate endowment grows into what we call a normal man, the bearer, and in part the victim, of the civilization that has been so painfully acquired.

I should like you to notice, too, that the analysis of dreams has shown us that the unconscious makes use of a particular symbolism which varies partly from individual to individual; but partly it is laid down in a typical form and seems to coincide with the symbolism which, as we suspect, underlies our myths and fairy tales. It seems not impossible that these creations of the popular mind might find an explanation through the help of dreams.

Lastly, I must warn you not to let yourselves be put out by the objection that the occurrence of anxiety-dreams contradicts our view of dreams as the fulfilments of wishes. Apart from the fact that these anxiety-dreams, like the rest, require interpreta-tion before any judgement can be formed on them, it must be stated quite generally that the anxiety does not depend on the content of the dream in such a simple manner as one might imagine without having more knowledge and taking more ac-count of the determinants of neurotic anxiety. Anxiety is one of the ego's reactions in repudiation of repressed wishes that have become powerful; and its occurrence in dreams as well is very easily explicable when the formation of the dream has been carried out with too much of an eye to the fulfilment of these repressed wishes.

As you see, research into dreams would be justified for its own sake merely by the information it gives us on matters that can with difficulty be discovered in other ways. But we were in fact led to the subject in connection with the psychoanalytic treatment of neurotics. . . .[26]

The impression which that passage may well have made upon his hearers could have been one of tantalizing glimpses. This may even have been Freud's intention; or it may have been the outcome of an unconscious wish on his part to take revenge for the humiliating neglect which his original treatise on the subject of the interpretation of dreams had received when it was first published. He had worked on it for a long time, and had withheld publication even longer. It was finally published on 4 November 1899, but dated 1900 by the publishers.

It might seem hard to conceive how a book, since recognized as one of the great classics of human thought, could achieve so disastrous and humiliating a fate in its first edition. The first printing was 600 copies: it took eight years to sell them. In the six weeks following publication 123 copies were sold, but only a further 228 were sold over the following two years. Yet this book is now universally regarded as Freud's greatest work: it set itself a dual task, a complete exposition of Freud's theory of dreams, and a confirmation of his earlier theories of unconscious mental mechanisms, brilliantly exemplified. Freud himself never doubted the importance of the book and of the discoveries therein recorded, which had changed his own life. His verdict upon it emerged in a special preface which he wrote for the English edition thirty-two years later.

This book, with the new contribution to psychology which surprised the world when it was published (1900), remains essentially unaltered. It contains, even according to my present-day judgement, the most valuable of all the discoveries which it has been my good fortune to make. Insight such as this falls to one's lot but once in a lifetime.[27]

However, not all the opposition to the book was the outcome of unconscious resistance on the part of the readers. A fascinating book for someone whose interest has already been aroused, it is nevertheless far less satisfying than the importance of its subject, and the transformation of its author after he had mastered that subject and completed the book, might have led one to expect.

Freud himself was well aware of the crucial difficulty which had faced him. Free association, which was the key to his interpretation of dreams, only allowed him to use for interpretation either dreams brought to him by his patients or those of his own dreams which he had analysed himself. He was reluctant to use only telling fragments of his anonymous patients' dreams, principally because the already familiar criticism levelled against his work was that it was based upon at best abnormal, at worst totally unbalanced, people. But when he came to recount his own dreams and their interpretation, he was continually obliged to limit what he said because of the demands of his own personal privacy. The critic Wittels observed that the outcome of this dilemma, in which Freud used fragments of the dreams of both his patients and himself, fragments and interpretations which were themselves often partial and inconclusive, was that 'Freud falls short in the very work which embodies the most fundamental of his discoveries'.

To overcome this difficulty without injustice to the remarkable originality and penetrating wisdom of Freud's observations, we can consider them in crystallized form, and take as illustrations one or two of Freud's own examples, together with some from his later pupils.

Freud said that all dreams were meaningful. Not only does the dream have a meaning but the meaning of the dream is the cause of the dream. What we remember of this dream is the manifest content, what causes the dream is the latent or repressed and unconscious content. There is an extremely complicated relationship between the two and this can only be uncovered by employing free association to every item of the manifest content, and thus getting back to the latent content.

The mechanisms which have served to change and distort the latent content into the manifest content were listed by Freud. He called them condensation, displacement, dramatization, symbolization and secondary elaboration. We shall later have something to say about each one of them. Meanwhile, we can take as our first example of a dream an illustration given by one of Freud's most brilliant pupils, Ferenczi.

One of his women patients dreamed one night that she was strangling a little white dog. There is nothing particularly impossible about this dream, but it puzzled her. She asked Ferenczi to analyse it for her. Her associations to the dream just as she had recalled it were that she liked cooking very much and that she often had to kill animals, to wring the necks of pigeons or chickens. She disliked doing that and so she did it as quickly as possible. At this point she remarked that in her dream she had strangled the dog in exactly the same way that she would strangle chickens in real life. She then went on to general speculations and phantasies about capital punishment, about the manner in which hanging is carried out and what it must feel like to be hanged. She seemed compelled to dwell on this sinister subject. Ferenczi then asked her if she had a particular grudge against anyone. She said yes she had, and added that it was against her sister-in-law. She went on, 'She is trying to come between my husband and myself, like a tame dove.' She began to realize the significance of her own train of thought, and then suddenly remembered a violent quarrel some days before in the course of which she had actually turned her sister-in-law out of the house saying, 'Get out, I don't want a dog that bites in my house!' Ferenczi adds that the interpretation of the dream was by now obvious to the dreamer. She added in confirmation that her sister-in-law was short and of a remarkably pale complexion.

We can follow this dream with one from Freud's own original collection, which is in many ways remarkably similar. Here it is in his own words:

'You're always saying to me,' began a clever woman patient of mine, 'that a dream is a fulfilled wish. Well, I'll tell you a dream whose subject was the exact opposite – a dream in which one of my wishes was not fulfilled. How do you fit that in with your theory? This was the dream:

'*I wanted to give a supper-party, but I had nothing in the house but a little smoked salmon. I thought I would go out and buy something, but remembered then that it was Sunday afternoon and all the shops would be shut. Next I tried to ring up some caterers, but the telephone was out of order. So I had to abandon my wish to give a supper-party.*'

I answered, of course, that analysis was the only way of deciding on the meaning of the dream; though I admitted that at first sight it seemed sensible and coherent and looked like the reverse of a wish-fulfilment. 'But what material did the dream arise from? As you know, the instigation to a dream is always to be found in the events of the previous day.'[28]

Despite the fact that the manifest content was indeed quite the opposite of the apparent wish fulfilment, the analysis revealed the true position. After some trivial remarks the patient explained that the day before she had visited a lady friend of whom she was very jealous, because she thought her husband admired the woman. Luckily the friend was thin, and her husband liked full figures. The friend spoke of her desire to get fat and, in the course of the conversation, said to the dreamer, 'When are you going to ask us over again? You always have such good food.' The meaning of the dream then became clear to the dreamer; it was exactly as though she had answered her friend, 'Oh indeed, so I am to invite you so that you can get a good meal and put on weight and become still more appealing to my husband! I'd sooner give no more supper-parties.' Freud pointed out that this dream was in fact the disguised fulfilment of a forbidden or repressed wish.

All dreams, said Freud, are fulfilments of wishes; most children's dreams are either direct wish fulfilments or compensations for wishes whose fulfilment has been blocked, frustrated or postponed in waking life. The dreams of adults are more complicated, because the restriction usually comes from within and has already been the subject of repression. Anxiety in dreams is often aroused even by the disguised fulfilment of a repressed wish, particularly if the original repression was necessary to spare the patient anguish, guilt, or apprehension.

We have yet to take account of Freud's deep but divided feelings for his father. He was severely affected by his father's death, and developed a number of symptoms which he himself privately regarded as hysterical. The night before his father's funeral he had a dream in which he saw a printed placard showing the sentence: 'You are requested to shut the eyes.' But on further reflection he was not sure that the placard might not have said: 'You are requested to shut one eye.' Someone with no experience in analysis might imagine that a choice had to be made between these sentences before free association could begin. Freud, on the contrary, sought the causes of the dream in both directions and found that they were the same. The sentence with the words 'shut the eyes' was evidently connected with the death of his father. His father's eyes were closed in death.

Freud also knew that there might be things about his relationship with his father to which he had always wished to shut his own eyes, but which had been stirred beneath the surface of consciousness by his father's death. He began to seek associations for the origin of the other sentence, the words 'shut one eye'. He remembered that he had decided that the funeral should be very simple, knowing his father's wishes on the subject. Some members of the family had disapproved of this, largely on the conventional grounds of what other people would say. Freud saw he had tried to turn a blind eye to this conflict in his family, to wink at it, to indulge in a compromise between the wishes of his dead father for a simple funeral and of some of his family for a more elaborate one. The two sentences are linked in the latent content of the dream and both expressed Freud's preoccupation on the subject of his father's death and funeral.

Understandably, but somewhat disconcertingly for the reader, Freud does not pursue this topic any farther: although neither he nor the reader are left in any doubt that the analysis itself must have gone farther, and must have uncovered material highly relevant to the deeply charged feelings which even then he could only partially acknowledge. Later in this book we shall see how those feelings coloured other aspects of his life and judgement and particularly his attitude towards political, religious and metaphysical speculation.

Meanwhile, we have come to the point where we can consider Freud's views upon the sources of dreams. He distinguished four specific ways in which a dream may originate.

(1) A recent and important fact of the dreamer's emotional life is directly represented in the dream. This is frequently self-evident, as in the simple wish-fulfilment dreams of children and, indeed, may require no interpretation.

(2) Several recent and important ideas are blended into a simple whole by the dream. Analysis is necessary here, but simply to resolve that aspect of the dream work which Freud calls 'condensation', and which will be our next concern.

(3) One or a number of recent and important events in a dreamer's emotional life may be represented in the dream by an equally recent but relatively indifferent memory. Here the mechanism has included what Freud called 'displacement'; more complicated analysis through free association will be necessary to uncover it.

(4) An important but long-past and buried memory or idea is represented in the dream by a recent and relatively indifferent impression. This is the most complex type of displacement, and occurs relatively more frequently in the dreams of those who are already exhibiting symptoms of emotional disturbance in their waking life.

It will be noticed that in every case Freud postulated that some part of the dream must be related to an event in the immediate past. He went so far as to say that this event would have occurred within the twenty-four hours immediately preceding the dream. Obviously, when the recent event is so trivial as to be otherwise unmemorable, only free association will bring it to light, and only further association will show its relevance to the more significant deeply repressed recent, or long-past, emotionally charged ideas.

What, then, is the dream work to which we have had occasion to refer and which Freud specified with some precision? The principal mechanisms have already been listed:

(1) Condensation.

(2) Displacement.

(3) Dramatization.

(4) Symbolization.

(5) Secondary elaboration.

We can consider each in turn.

(1) *Condensation*

Dreams are brief, meagre and laconic in comparison with the range and wealth of the dream-thoughts.[29]

This expresses the essence of condensation. It means that in the manifest dream, one idea can stand for a great many associations which, in turn, will lead to quite separate although frequently overlapping ideas in the latent content. To this process, whereby one recognizable idea or memory stands in fact for a number of previously unrecognizable, far more important and apparently unrelated, ideas or memories, Freud gave the special name 'over-determination'. His own examples in *The Interpretation of Dreams* are vivid but extremely complicated, but a dream of one of a colleague's patients again supplies a simpler but equally vivid example. This one is reported by Frink.

A young American woman dreamed that she was walking on Fifth Avenue with a friend, looking for a new hat. Finally she went in and bought one. This apparently trivial recollection was the total content of the manifest dream as remembered by the dreamer. Association and analysis led to the following data.

The walk with the friend the previous day had actually taken place, and had indeed been along Fifth Avenue. There had however been no question of the purchase of a new hat. Moving on from this the dreamer said that in fact her husband had been ill in bed that day. The illness was only a trivial and transient one, but she had been worried by her private preoccupation with the possibility of her husband's death. When her friend called, her husband, who had noticed her quietness and apparent gloom, had suggested that she and her friend should go out together to get out of the house for a bit. During their walk, the dreamer had found herself discussing a man whom she had known before her marriage. At this point her associations ceased. Frink asked her to go on, and eventually she said that this was a man with whom she had at one time thought she was in love. Frink asked her if she had ever considered marrying this man. She then laughed unhappily and said that he had never asked her, and that their financial and social positions had been so different that it would be fantastic even to dream of it. Despite this revelation, she was still unable to associate further to the idea of this man, and her next association concerned buying the hat. She then admitted that she was very partial to hats, and would like to have bought many, but in fact she and her husband could not afford this kind of expenditure. At this point she suddenly remembered that the hat she had bought in the dream had been a black hat. 'It was a mourning hat . . .' she added. This final detail began to make the whole dream clear.[30]

Freud himself has commented that, in the midst of the interpretation, a previously omitted fragment of a dream frequently emerges, and the dreamer at once says that until this instant it had been entirely forgotten.

This part of the dream which has been wrested from forgetfulness is always the most important part. It lies on the shortest path to the solution of the dream, and it is for that very reason it was most exposed to the resistance. . . .[31]

(*Interpretation of Dreams*)

Frink's interpretation of his patient's dream was as follows:

The day before the dream the patient had feared that her husband might die. That night she dreamed that she had bought a mourning hat, which suggested a forbidden wish for her husband's death, which had troubled her as an irrational anxiety in the daytime, and had then emerged as part of the latent content of the dream. In her waking life she could not have afforded a new hat; in the dream she bought one without hesitation. This implied that she was better off, as indeed she would have been if she had married the man with whom she had first been in love. It emerged from the dream that in fact the woman had not only wished that she had married the first man, but had believed that despite the social difference which had seemed decisive to her, he too had wanted to marry her. Neither of them had ever got to the point of doing anything about it. The condensation in the dream is of three different repressed wishes, all of them disguised, all of them forbidden by her real circumstances, to which consciously she was reconciled. She wished she were free to marry the first man, which would imply that she wanted her husband out of the way. She wished she were free to spend the money which this other marriage would have made available to her, and in spending it, she signified both the change in her marital and financial position, and the ending of her actual husband's claims and need of her, by his death.[32]

When the patient discussed this with Frink she acknowledged that every aspect of it was true, and that in the past few weeks she had often thought about the first man whom she might have married. The over-determination here is represented by the buying of the mourning hat. Beneath it there lies the three-fold wish: for her husband's death, for her to have married the man she first loved and for her to have plenty of money.

Another aspect of this dream which accords perfectly with

Freud's views is the capacity of unconscious images to correspond to several wishes, which in real life would have been contradictory or mutually exclusive. If her husband were dead and she had married her first love, the hat she bought would not have been a mourning hat.

(2) *Displacement*

This is a process whereby the emotional charge is separated from its real object or content and attached to an entirely different one. It is this that enables a dream whose manifest content is apparently trivial to be accompanied by great feelings of anxiety or excitement or, conversely, for a dream in which apparently terrible or important things happen to be recounted with very little conscious involvement of emotion at all. Examples of this can be taken from dreams already quoted. In the dream of the strangling of the little white dog, the emotion of resentment, even of murderous hatred, is displaced from the image of the sister-in-law on to that of the animal; one important result of this is that the image of the sister-in-law does not appear in the manifest dream at all. In the dream of the purchase of the mourning hat, the walk, itself relatively unimportant, is the first thing the dreamer remembers, and the buying of the hat comes at the end and is almost left out. The memory that the hat was black, which contains the key to the whole emotional background of the dream, only emerges once free association and analysis have begun.

A final case from Frink will provide an even more telling example. One of his patients was a girl suffering from an obsessional neurosis, who dreamed that she was in the presence of someone whom she couldn't identify, but who seemed important to her. She wanted to give him something and what she gave him was her comb. Once again this was all she could relate as the manifest content of the dream and, surprisingly enough, it seemed to mean nothing to her.

Analysis had already revealed an important part of her history. She was a Jewess who wanted to marry a Protestant, but the family were strictly orthodox, and the rule against marrying out had prevented this. She herself had believed that there was no real obstacle to a mixed marriage, but what had prevented her had been the recognition that, if they had married and had children, there might have been conflicts about the religious upbringing of the children and, indeed, the children themselves might have suffered from such disharmony, or from the attitude of the strictly orthodox grandparents towards children of a mixed marriage. She had therefore rejected her lover's proposal of marriage, very much against her own inclinations, and privately blaming her parents and his for this impasse. The night before the dream she had in fact had a violent quarrel with her mother. While going to bed and combing out her hair, she had been thinking about leaving home altogether, for her own and her parents' sake, and considering how she would support herself if she did.

Her associations began with the word 'comb'. She suddenly remembered a phrase heard in her childhood and, until then, entirely forgotten. She had been about to comb her hair with somebody else's comb. The person had said to her, 'Don't do that, you will mix the breed.' The latent content of the dream was released with quite spectacular impact. She realized that the person in the dream had been the man she wanted to marry, although this recognition had previously been impossible for her; by offering him her comb, she was showing her wish to mix the breed, in fact to marry him and bear his children, despite parental opposition and despite her acknowledgement of it by renouncing the prospect of marriage. So what had seemed to be an almost meaninglessly unimportant dream had really expressed an extremely important intention. Displacement had removed the idea of marrying the man from the manifest content, and replaced it by the initially incomprehensible symbolic act of giving him her comb.

Until the analytic procedure is given its chance the dream remains apparently meaningless, and indeed curiously or, as Freud would say, significantly vague. But all this apparent triviality is in fact the effect of condensation and displacement. This leads us to anticipate what Freud was later to introduce into the concept of the dream work, namely the function of censorship. It is exactly as though manifest dreams were smuggled messages in code, of the kind used in war to convey secret meanings to resistance movements within an enemy-occupied country. Decoding them gives hitherto apparently trivial or meaningless phrases their true significance. Similarly, war correspondents, sending back dispatches from areas where a censorship is operating, may adopt such devices to get their news through. The dream work alters latent to manifest content to evade, while seeming to conform to, what remains of the censorship. We shall have more to say about Freud's concept of the censor towards the end of this chapter.

The remaining mechanisms are now easily understandable.

(3) *Dramatization*

By far the greatest part of remembered dreams are vivid visual images. Conceptual thought is often absent, however, or is only introduced into the account of the dream if the dreamer ventures to put it into words. If motion pictures had existed when Freud was writing *The Interpretation of Dreams* they would have provided him with the precise analogy for dramatization by visual imagery which he considered characteristic of dreams. As it was he had to use more ancient and traditional comparisons.

The incapacity of dreams to express these things must lie in the nature of the psychical material out of which dreams are made. The plastic arts of painting and sculpture labour, indeed, under a similar limitation as compared with poetry, which can make

use of speech; and here once again the reason for their incapacity lies in the nature of the material which these two forms
of art manipulate in their effort to express something.[33]

Freud had been struck by the way in which the visual
imagery of dreams, although often vivid, complicated and
manifestly inexplicable, seems to present ideas without having
any way of communicating the relationship between them. The
ideas, the feelings, the total of the dream remain without logic
or explicit connexion. Every picture tells a story; but the
pictures in dreams do not tell the story of the dream in terms of
what it really means. This is why nothing but free association
and an understanding of symbolization can uncover the truth.
Nevertheless, the sequence of visual images certainly produces
a connected experience which, while the dream lasts, seems to
be valid. It is only when the dream is recalled after waking that
its manifest absurdity and, sometimes, its almost incom-
municable mysteriousness, become evident to the dreamer.
The dramatic sequence of the dream, linked with the unex-
pressed relationships which only interpretation can uncover, is
what Freud called 'dramatization'. It is as though the dreamer
were both watching and involved in a mystery play, a problem
picture or a challenging and disturbing, although overtly incomprehensible, film. Symbolization provides the one standard
clue to what is happening, as opposed to the individual and
personal clue of free association.

(4) *Symbolization*

One of the simplest and most vivid examples Freud ever gave
of visual imagery in a dream dramatizing a latent wish to evade
repression was when he told of a man who had dreamed *that his
brother was digging up his garden all over again*. The dreamer's
first association was to deep trenching for vegetables; his
second gave the meaning of the dream. The brother was *re-
trenching*. (Re-trenching his expenses.) But in fact the brother

was not doing this at all. The latent meaning of the dream was that the dreamer *wished* that his brother *would* cut down his expenses, because he was worried about the responsibilities which might come his way if a financial catastrophe overtook the brother. This was a meaning which only free association could obtain, and which was personal to the dreamer. Symbolization is a different kind of distortion, but with a similar link to latent content. Freud's own words about this were:

Symbolism is perhaps the most remarkable chapter of the theory of dreams. In the first place, since symbols are stable translations, they realize to some extent the ideal of the ancient as well as of the popular interpretation of dreams, from which, with our technique, we had departed widely. They allow us in certain circumstances to interpret a dream without questioning the dreamer, who indeed would in any case have nothing to tell us about the symbol. If we are acquainted with the ordinary dream-symbols, and in addition with the dreamer's personality, the circumstances in which he lives and the impressions which preceded the occurrence of the dream, we are often in a position to interpret a dream straightaway . . .

Interpretation based on a knowledge of symbols is not a technique which can replace or compete with the associative one. It forms a supplement to the latter. . . .[34]

Freud leads up to the sexual symbolism of dreams with circumspection, but once embarked on it he becomes direct.

The male genitals, then, are represented in dreams in a number of ways that must be called symbolic, where the common element in the comparison is mostly very obvious. To begin with, for the male genitals as a whole the sacred number 3 is of symbolic significance. The more striking and for both sexes the more interesting component of the genitals, the male organ, finds symbolic substitutes in the first instance in things that resemble it in shape – things, accordingly, that are long and up-standing, such as *sticks, umbrellas, posts, trees* and so on; further, in objects which share with the thing they represent the characteristic of penetrating into the body and injuring – thus, sharp *weapons* of every kind, *knives, daggers, spears, sabres,* but also fire-arms, *rifles, pistols* and *revolvers* (particularly suitable owing to their shape). In the anxiety dreams of girls, being followed by a man with a knife or a fire-arm plays a large part. This is perhaps the commonest instance of dream-symbolism and you will now be able to translate it easily. Nor is there any difficulty in understanding how it is that the male organ can be replaced by objects from which water flows – *water-taps, watering-cans,* or *fountains* – or again by other objects which are capable of being lengthened, such as hanging-lamps, extensible pencils, etc. A no less obvious aspect of the organ explains the fact that *pencils, pen-holders, nail-files, hammers,* and other *instruments* are undoubted male sexual symbols.

The remarkable characteristic of the male organ which enables it to rise up in defiance of the laws of gravity, one of the phenomena of erection, leads to its being represented symbolically by *balloons, flying-machines* and most recently by *zeppelin airships.* But dreams can symbolize erection in yet another, far more expressive manner. They can treat the sexual organ as the essence of the dreamer's whole person and make him himself *fly.* Do not take it to heart if dreams of flying, so familiar and often so delightful, have to be interpreted as dreams of general sexual excitement, as erection-dreams. . . . And do not make an objection out of the fact that women can have the same flying dreams as men. Remember, rather, that our dreams aim at being the fulfilments of wishes and that the wish to be a man is found so frequently, consciously or unconsciously, in women. Nor will anyone with a knowledge of anatomy be bewildered by the fact that it is possible for women to realize this wish through the same sensations as men. Women possess as part of their genitals a small organ similar to the male one; and this small organ, the clitoris, actually plays the same part in childhood and during the years before sexual intercourse as the large organ in men.

Among the less easily understandable male sexual symbols are certain *reptiles* and *fishes,* and above all the famous symbol of the *snake.* It is certainly not easy to guess why *hats* and *overcoats* or *cloaks* are employed in the same way, but their symbolic significance is quite unquestionable. And finally we can ask ourselves whether the replacement of the male limb by another limb, the foot or the hand, should be described as symbolic. We are, I think, compelled to do so by the context and by counterparts in the case of women.

The female genitals are symbolically represented by all such objects as share their characteristic of enclosing a hollow space which can take something into itself: by *pits*, *cavities* and *hollows*, for instance, by *vessels* and *bottles*, by *receptacles*, *boxes*, *trunks*, *cases*, *chests*, *pockets*, and so on. *Ships*, too, fall into this category. Some symbols have more connection with the uterus than with the female genitals: thus, *cupboards*, *stoves* and, more especially, *rooms*. Here room-symbolism touches on house-symbolism. *Doors* and *gates*, again, are symbols of the genital orifice. Materials, too, are symbols for women: *wood*, *paper* and objects made from them, like *tables* and *books*. Among animals, *snails* and *mussels* at least are undeniably female symbols; among parts of the body, the *mouth* (as a substitute for the genital orifice); among buildings, *churches* and *chapels*. Not every symbol, as you will observe, is equally intelligible. . . .[35]

Freud gives a great many more of these symbols and then confronts his readers with the objections which he is sure must have by now occurred to them.

Here, then, is material used for symbolism in dreams. It is not complete and could be carried deeper as well as further. But I fancy it will seem to you more than enough and may even have exasperated you. 'Do I really live in the thick of sexual symbols?' you may ask. 'Are all the objects around me, all the clothes I put on, all the things I pick up, all of them sexual symbols and nothing else?' There is really ground enough for raising astonishing questions, and, as a first one, we may enquire how we in fact come to know the meaning of these dream-symbols, upon which the dreamer himself gives us insufficient information or none at all.

My reply is that we learn from very different sources – from fairy tales and myths, from buffoonery and jokes, from folklore (that is, from knowledge about popular manners and customs, sayings and songs) and from poetic and colloquial linguistic usage. In all these directions we come upon the same symbolism, and in some of them we can understand it without further instruction. If we go into these sources in detail, we shall find so many parallels to dream-symbolism that we cannot fail to be convinced of our interpretations.[36]

As well as dreams of flying, Freud included climbing ladders and staircases, mounting horses, and even sometimes walking or running as symbols of sexual intercourse, giving examples from language to show the recognition of this sexual significance; for example the word *steigen*, in German, meaning 'to mount', being directly represented in the phrases '*Den Frauen nachsteigen*' (to run after women) and '*ein alter steiger*' (an old roué). So, in French, where the word for 'step' is *la marche*, we find the quite analogous expression for an old rake: '*un vieux marcheur*'. Probably the fact that with many of the larger animals sexual intercourse necessitates a mounting or 'climbing upon' the female has something to do with this association of ideas.

'Pulling off a branch' as a symbolic representation of masturbation is not merely in harmony with vulgar descriptions of the act but has far-reaching mythological parallels.[37]

After completing his account of the symbolism of dreams, Freud returned again to his all-too-well-founded apprehension that this would arouse tremendous resistance and opposition in many of his hearers and readers. In one way he understood this; in another he still found it puzzling that even professional colleagues should be so outraged by what he had to say, whereas the existence of such symbolism in myths, religion, art and language was not only beyond all doubt but unreservedly accepted by all educated people.

. . . it must strike you that the symbolism in the other fields I have mentioned is by no means solely sexual symbolism, whereas in dreams symbols are used almost exclusively for the expression of sexual objects and relations.[38]

(5) *Secondary Elaboration*

This is the easiest of the mechanisms of the dream work to understand. It is simply the outcome of the dreamer's natural tendency on waking to make some sort of sense, to himself, of his recollection of the dream. Freud was never tired of emphasizing that, in interpreting dreams, it was not simply useless but actually misleading to attempt to explain one part of the manifest dream by another part, as though the dream were a coherent conception. Dramatization and symbolization referred to the latent content, and bore no necessary logical relationship to the manifest content at all. However, such a completely chaotic but vivid jumble of ideas, thoughts, feelings, fragmented or distorted memories, and emotionally charged experiences defies recollection or description in the actual form in which it is experienced during the dream.

Most of us, when recalling, and even more when recounting, our own dreams, are aware that we are compelled to undertake some degree of secondary elaboration to make them capable of expression in words, let alone communicable in any way which satisfies our sense of narrative, order or significance. The fact that some secondary elaboration is an indispensable part of the human attempt to deal with the manifest content of the dream during waking life simply adds one more element of distortion to the latent content, of which the manifest content is merely the disguised, distorted expression.

We can now grasp the remarkable concept of the nature and interpretation of dreams as worked out by Freud, and its vital importance to the entire theory and practice of psychoanalysis. The dream is a disguised and distorted expression of a repressed and forbidden wish. The total distortion occurs through the mechanisms of the dream work, and is part of the price still remaining to be paid when unconscious material struggles through to consciousness, even in the altered physiological and psychological conditions of sleep. Freud regards the biological purpose of the dream as the preservation of sleep. It permits ideas and feelings to be worked through which otherwise would disturb sleep, just as dreaming will also permit stimuli, which would otherwise arouse the dreamer, to be experienced without his waking. The examples of the alarm clock or the telephone which are heard in the dream as part of the dream but do not, at least at first, succeed in waking the sleeper, because they are accepted as part of the dream experience, are illustrations of this.

From the psychological standpoint, however, the function of the dream is to discharge the tensions of the repressed and forbidden wish. If these are extreme, the dream will be charged with anxiety, and indeed the process may be unsuccessful and the sleeper may wake, probably feeling and displaying the signs of anxiety and disturbance appropriate to the threatening but repressed emotion. However, if the dream succeeds in protecting sleep, the compromise between repression and the return of the repressed material will be complete. The dream work will have succeeded and the manifest content of the dream will be relatively tolerable to the sleeper, even though the latent content still escapes conscious recognition. Sometimes, when the resistance to the emergence of this material exerted by Freud's concept of the censorship is extreme, *the dream itself may actually be censored.* Freud gives one classic example of this from the dream of a middle-aged woman, who was consulting a pupil of his, Dr Hug-Hellmuth. A condensed version of the dream, and the remarkably concise comment of the meaning of the term 'censor' are taken from Dalbiez' classical treatise, *Psychoanalytical Method and the Doctrine of Freud:*

A woman aged fifty, the widow of an officer of high rank who had died twelve years before, had the following dream in 1915, at a time when one of her sons was at the front: She goes to the military hospital and asks the sentry at the door for the surgeon in charge, as she wishes to offer her services in the hospital. The noncommissioned officer understands, from the emphasis which she lays on the word 'services', that she means love-services; he hesitates, but lets her pass. She enters a large room, in which a number of officers and doctors are sitting round a table. She makes her offer to a staff-surgeon: 'I and many other women and young girls of Vienna are ready to . . . (*still dreaming, she hears a murmur*) . . . the soldiers, officers and privates without distinction.' For a moment there is a painful silence. The staff-surgeon puts his arm round her and says, 'Dear lady, imagine if it actually came to . . . (*again she hears a murmur*) . . .' She withdraws from his arm thinking 'One is just like another,' and replies: 'My God, I'm an old woman, and shall perhaps never be in that position. Besides, one condition must be made: there is the consideration of age; an old woman must not . . . (*here too she hears a murmur*) . . . a mere lad; that would be terrible.' The staff-surgeon: 'I understand perfectly'; then he shows her the staircase which leads to the surgeon in charge. While she is climbing it, with the feeling that she is simply doing her duty, she hears an officer say: 'This is a tremendous decision, whether a woman is young or old; all honour to her.'

This dream, so coherent and unified, presents one striking characteristic: the three most indelicate passages are replaced, *in the dream itself*, by a murmur. Freud sees in this something more than a meaningless chance, and refuses to admit that it is simply a case of coincidence. In his view, the lady's moral feelings have continued to exist during sleep, though in a weakened form, and have produced a characteristic disturbance at the most offensive points of the dream. Thus mutilated, the dream is like those newspapers printed during the war, in which a blank space stood for the passages deleted by the censor. Sometimes the journalist, foreseeing censorship, used to introduce circumlocutions and obscurities into his report. Freud believes that the suppression of the three most indecent passages in the dream of the fifty-year-old widow is an effect-sign of the existence of a true endo-psychic censor.

What is to be understood by the censor? No entity is meant. The censor simply denotes the sum of the urges which prevail in the consciousness of a given individual, in so far as the said urges exercise an inhibitory function upon the urges opposed to them, which they drive back into the unconscious. It must, however, be noted that in Freud's view this inhibitory function is only consciously exercised in very early life; it soon becomes automatic, then unconscious, and repression takes the place of suppression. Not only does the censor consign to the unconscious the urges which oppose it and which have penetrated into consciousness, but its inhibitory power is exercised even before their entry into consciousness. This is one of Freud's most highly original concepts. Since then, he has modified his formulas and his terminology: the super-ego has taken the place of the censor. . . .[39]

We are not yet ready to consider Freud's concept of the super-ego, which has as much to do with his theory of conscience as with repression. What is important is to realize that even in sleep repressed thoughts have to pass the barrier of censorship before they can return even to the twilight consciousness of dreaming.

Finally, there is one illustration which Freud himself used. It was one more of his strenuous efforts to make people realize that the manifest content of the dream *was not in itself to be expected to make sense, to be coherent, or necessarily to illustrate directly any aspect of the latent content whatsoever*. The more the dream work succeeds in separating manifest and latent content, the more incomprehensible will the manifest dream be and, therefore, the more indispensable the reversal or undoing of the dream work becomes. The technique of this reversal is simply free association to each separate item of the dream, and the understanding of the specific symbolic language common in varying degree to all dreams. Freud's most telling illustration of this way of considering the manifest dream was to liken it to one of those symbolic visual puzzles, in his day called a *rebus*, and still occasionally encountered in children's papers today. This will be easier to understand from English linguistic examples invented by the author, rather than the original German examples necessarily used by Freud.

Imagine three pictures in a magazine which you are invited to interpret as part of a readers' competition. The first picture shows a wide scene of ascending steps, carpeted and with a balustrade on either side. The second picture shows a familiar four-legged animal with wool on its back, a black face and two curved horns, charging towards the wooden entrance to the field, bounded by railings, in which it is enclosed. The third picture is of a crowd of people surrounding an object which looks like a large pebble or smooth rock. These pictures have no significance as works of art, nor do they appear to have any meaningful relationship one to another. But the clue in the competition is provided by the information that they each represent the name of an English seaside town. Once this principle is grasped it is not difficult to recognize that the first stands for Broadstairs, the second for Ramsgate and the third for Folkestone.

The manifest content of the dream is like the picture; and it would be as irrelevant and futile to criticize either the apparent absurdity, or the inconsequence, of remembered dreams as it would to become involved in an assessment of the artistic merit or intellectual content of the pictures in the puzzle. In both cases the interpretation can only be made by understanding and accepting the rules and the procedure, which govern the way in which the images have been produced. It was remarkable how few people who read Freud's original work were prepared to make this imaginative concession, still less to try the experiments which were clearly outlined in order to verify his findings for themselves. Once again, he attributed this intransigence to their resistance to the sexual aspects of his theories.

The most familiar form of calumny to which this resistance has given rise is that ' Freud says everything is due to sex '. This he never said; but, as with most wild and emotional statements, it contains elements of both truth and falsehood. We shall unravel both before this book is over. As far as dreams were concerned, Freud never maintained that all dreams had a sexual meaning. He readily acknowledged that some dreams are provoked by needs which have no sexual element, such as hunger or thirst. Moreover he several times formally protested against this misrepresentation:

The assertion that all dreams require a sexual interpretation, against which critics rage so incessantly, occurs nowhere in my *Interpretation of Dreams*. It is not to be found in any of the numerous editions of this book and is in obvious contradiction to other views expressed in it. I have already shown elsewhere that strikingly innocent dreams may embody crudely erotic wishes, and I could confirm this by many new instances. But it is also true that many dreams which appear to be indifferent and which one would not regard as in any respect peculiar lead back on analysis to wishful impulses which are unmistakably sexual and often of an unexpected sort.[40]

However, here as in practically everything else he wrote, he tried to be fair to his critics as well as to himself:

The more one is concerned with the solution of dreams, the more one is driven to recognize that the majority of the dreams of adults deal with sexual material and give expression to erotic wishes.[41]

Freud was a sensitive and kindly man, despite the image of himself which he often sought to convey as a detached and unemotional scientist. It had become his fate to feel like Cassandra, a prophet whose message was constantly and seemingly wilfully misunderstood. One effect on him of this experience was to impel him to insist even more emphatically upon his ideas, in the form in which he had attempted steadily and reasonably to expound them. The final quotation in this context returns to the theme of the difference between the latent

and the manifest content of dreams; and the sensitive reader
will detect a ring of poignancy rather than of pedantry about it:

I hope you will never again confuse these two things with each
other. If you reach that point, you will probably have gone
further in understanding dreams than most readers of my
Interpretation of Dreams.[42]

The title of this chapter is taken from a book which Freud published in 1901, and which was devoted to the study of trivial errors, omissions, slips of the tongue, etc., in everyday life. Freud considered that these occurrences were not examples of random chance operating freely in human life but were in fact symbolic of unconscious attitudes. Like dreams, such apparently chance errors, omissions and slips had a meaning and, as with dreams, this meaning could only be discovered by the psychoanalytic method of free association; but once discovered, it was clear and indisputable, at least to the insight of the author of the act, omission or error.

Three main categories of such errors, omissions or slips of the tongue can be distinguished:

(1) Where an emotional urge is released without repression; this is in fact a symptomatic act.

(2) Where an emotional urge is incompletely repressed, and there is a disturbed act.

(3) Where an emotional urge is completely repressed, and the act is inhibited.

An example of the first type of act can be quoted from Jean-Jacques Rousseau. In his *Sixième Promenade* Rousseau noted that he had acquired the habit of making a detour when approaching a certain boulevard. He wondered why. He eventually discovered that it was to avoid a little beggar whose chatter he disliked. 'We have no mechanical impulse,' writes Rousseau, 'the cause of which may not be found in our hearts, if we but knew how to seek it there.'[43] The French writer Claparède quotes this in his introduction to a French edition of Freud's work, and adds:

Substitute 'unconscious' for 'heart' and you have the very purest essence of the psychoanalytical doctrine.[44]

Freud's point was that examples of this kind not only occur to all of us but are susceptible of explanation based on an unconsciously determined mechanism. He instanced numerous examples of errors of this kind, to which he gave the general name of 'parapraxes'. These included stumbling, when one was in fact punishing oneself for apparently irrational anger or exasperation with somebody else, and leaving one's umbrella behind in a house to which one either felt obliged, or secretly wished, to return again. Losing or mislaying objects was of special interest to Freud because of the numerous meanings such actions might have and the way in which they might so readily be analysed.

All cases have in common the fact that there was a wish to lose something; they differ in the basis and aim of that wish. We lose a thing when it is worn out, when we intend to replace it by a better one, when we no longer like it, when it originates from someone with whom we are no longer on good terms or when we acquired it in circumstances we no longer want to recall. Dropping, damaging or breaking the object can serve the same purpose. In the sphere of social life experience is said to have shown that unwanted and illegitimate children are far more frail than those legitimately conceived. The crude technique of baby-farmers is not necessary for bringing about this result; a certain amount of neglect in looking after the children should be quite sufficient. The preserving of *things* may be subject to the same influences as that of children.

Things may, however, be condemned to be lost without their value having suffered any diminution – when, that is, there is an intention to sacrifice something to Fate in order to ward off some other dreaded loss. Analysis tells us that it is still quite a common thing among us to exorcize Fate in this way; and thus our losing is often a voluntary sacrifice. In the same way, losing may also serve the purpose of defiance or self-punishment. In short, the more remote reasons for the intention to get rid of a thing by losing it are beyond number.

Bungled actions, like other errors, are often used to fulfil wishes which one ought to deny oneself. Here the intention disguises itself as a lucky accident. For instance, as happened to one of my friends, a man may be due, obviously against his will, to go by train to visit someone near the town where he lives, and then, at a junction where he has to change, may by mistake get into a train that takes him back to where he came from. Or someone on a journey may be anxious to make a stop at an intermediate station but may be forbidden from doing so by other obligations, and he may then overlook or miss some connection so that he is after all obliged to break his journey in the way he wished. Or what happened to one of my patients: I had forbidden him to telephone to the girl he was in love with, and then, when he meant to telephone to me, he asked for the wrong number 'by mistake' or 'while he was thinking of something else' and suddenly found himself connected to the girl's number. . . .[45]

An example from Freud's own childhood will serve to illustrate the nature of a disturbed act, due to partial but incomplete repression. Somewhere between the age of two and a half and three Freud remembered himself weeping in front of a chest while his half-brother was holding the lid open. In the middle of this curious scene his mother entered the room. Freud at once ceased weeping and was comforted. Analysing this forty years later, he recalled that his mother looked very slim when she came into the room, that he had not seen her for some time, and that the cause of his distress had been that he believed that she was shut up in the chest and therefore had insisted that his half-brother, some ten years older than he, should open it for him.

Analysing further associations and dreams from that stage of his life, Freud then recalled that there had been a nursemaid in the house about that time who had asked him to entrust all his childhood savings to her. He could see no connexion

between this and the previous memory and finally asked his
mother whether she remembered the occasion. She said that
she did, and that the nursemaid had ultimately been discovered by the half-brother to have been stealing from the
house. She had been charged and arrested by the police. Most
of the stealing had occurred while Freud's mother was under-
going her confinement for the birth of Freud's younger sister.

At this point Freud himself was able to complete the memory
by recalling that the world 'confinement' had been used in two
quite different meanings in his hearing when he was barely
three: ŏnce referring to his mother's confinement, and the
second time referring to the reason for the disappearance of the
nursemaid – arrested and confined at the police station. When
his brother had been born, Freud had once again been excluded
from his mother's presence for her confinement, and had
imagined that this confinement was literal; that she was in fact
locked up somewhere in the house. This was why he urged his
half-brother to open the chest for him, and his memory of his
mother's slenderness may well have been connected with the
fact that she had changed a good deal in shape, even to his
child's eye, between the final stage of her pregnancy and her
reappearance after delivery.

What we have already seen in the *Interpretation of Dreams*
leads us straight to the heart of the matter, and so to recognize
what Freud had uncovered forty years after the event, by his
own analysis. There had been no rational grounds for his fear
that his mother might be shut up in the chest; nor, in retrospect, could he be certain that he had really thought that she
was there. *What he did know was that once again something had
taken her away from him, which he felt forbidden to understand.*
He leaves us to speculate about how much a child could
possibly have known of the sexual and biological aspects of the
birth of one of his siblings; but there is certainly no doubt that
this was a very disturbing event, and that the expression of this
disturbance suffered a classical displacement. He wept from

the anxious jealousy of his separation from his mother, not for the first time; and in his weeping he rationalized the cause as something immediate and at least open to investigation – his mother's confinement in the chest – rather than as something which experience had shown him he would not be allowed to investigate.

This piece of Freud's self-analysis also reminds us of the existence of screen memories, of which it is a perfect example. He remembers only the event which covered the ultimate cause of his anxiety; not the real nature of the anxiety itself. But its effect was behaviour which must have struck his mother as remarkable, and which he himself would certainly at that time have been unable to explain.

He gives us a more recent example from his practice:

A young woman who wore the breeches in her home, told me that her sick husband had been to the doctor to ask what diet he ought to follow for his health. The doctor, however, had said that a special diet was not important. She added: 'He can eat and drink what *I* want.'[46]

The slip here indicates the partial discharge of an incompletely repressed emotional urge: in this case, the woman's determination to dominate her husband, without acknowledging it.

An example of the third type of parapraxis, a completely repressed act, can again be given directly from Freud's own writing:

I set store by high-quality blotting paper (*Löschpapier*) and I decided one day to buy a fresh supply that afternoon in the course of my walk to the Inner Town. But I forgot for four days running, till I asked myself what reason I had for the omission. It was easy to find after I had recalled that though I normally write '*Löschpapier*' I usually say '*Fliesspapier*' (another word for 'blotting paper'). 'Fliess' is the name of a friend in Berlin who had on the days in question given me occasion for a worrying and anxious thought. I could not rid myself of this thought, but the defensive tendency manifested itself by transferring itself, by means of the verbal similarity, to the indifferent intention which on account of its indifference offered little resistance.[47]

This instance occurred at the time when Freud was repeating the pattern of his separation from Breuer with his later confidant and father-figure, Fliess. Some of Freud's repressed anxiety about Fliess was due to his knowledge that their separation had come about through acts on Freud's part of which he had some cause to be ashamed; and that a friendship which had meant so much to him had been repudiated in ways which conflicted with his own concept of himself as an entirely open-minded and honourable man. It was characteristic of him that he should not have spared himself, or his readers, this instance of the effect of a repressed conflict in an area which continued to trouble him.

Freud did not claim to be the sole originator of the observations contained in *The Psychopathology of Everyday Life*. Indeed he quoted Darwin and Nietzsche in support of his own observations. Darwin had written in his autobiography:

I had during years followed a golden rule, namely, whenever I came across a published fact, a new observation or idea, which ran counter to my general results, I made a memorandum of it without fail and at once; for I had found by experience that such facts and ideas were far more apt to slip the memory than favourable ones.

Nietzsche has expressed the same idea in a striking manner in his *Beyond Good and Evil*:

'I have done that,' says my memory. 'It is impossible that I should have done it,' says my pride, and it remains inexorable. Finally my memory yields.[48]

The Psychopathology of Everyday Life was Freud's first popular book, in the sense that it was written as much for laymen as for professional colleagues and scientists. It was not central to the practice of psychoanalysis, although it was by no means irrelevant to it. Most of its observations had to do with the field of memory and recognition, rather than with the alteration of other faculties such as physical sensation or motor power in the body. But in fact there is no reason for distinguishing between these faculties in terms of the impact of the effect of repressed emotional urges upon them. Slips of memory, and their subsequent effects, are observable in all of us: whereas loss of physical sensation or of motor power normally occur only in those suffering from hysterical symptoms; and we have already seen how readily hostility is experienced and expressed towards hysterical suffering by those who can neither accept its validity nor tolerate its manifestations.

There is indeed a striking difference in the usual social attitude, whereby failure, inhibition or distortion of memory are regarded as comparatively normal, whereas comparable loss or distortion of motor or sensory function are regarded not simply as pathological but all too often as disgraceful, unless they can be shown to have a demonstrably structural cause. Freud never confused this issue himself; he always regarded the distinction as entirely artificial and maintained that the same psychological mechanisms operated in the healthy as in the sick. The difference was in degree and not in kind. There is therefore a direct link between his studies in *The Psychopathology of Everyday Life* and his further contribution to the study of the neuroses which will concern us in Chapter 7.

From what has already been set out, it is clear that Freud had collected a great deal of information about the inner emotional lives of his patients, through the medium of psychoanalysis, by the time he had completed his work on the interpretation of dreams. His next major work was an apparent digression: an entire book *On the Nature of Jokes, and their Relation to the Unconscious*. Laborious in execution but enlivened by its discernment, it pursues the theme of the dynamic unconscious mechanisms underlying wit and humour. Throughout the communication of the human race, jokes endorse both the existence and the role of the unconscious as Freud had perceived it. The funniest jokes are often subtle allusions to crude themes, codes making possible reference to forbidden subjects, and therefore one might expect that sexual jokes would be the most compulsively popular of all. This, of course, is undoubtedly true. Nevertheless we must postpone Freud's concern with jokes until the latter part of this book, to consider first his next serious contribution to scientific thought, the famous *Three Essays on the Theory of Sexuality*.

The *Three Essays* will always remain one of Freud's major works. They provide the foundation for his theory of neuroses, the explanation of the need for repression and the source of emotional energy underlying conscious and unconscious drives and behaviour which he named *libido*. He did not expect them to be readily accepted, indeed he knew in advance that they would be resisted, denied and distorted, no matter what he did to convey them lucidly, cogently and explicitly. Together with *The Interpretation of Dreams*, this was one of the publications which he constantly revised and brought up to date throughout successive editions. Later in his life, in *The Introductory*

Lectures to Psychoanalysis, and in his final and not quite completed work *An Outline of Psychoanalysis,* he altered the order of presentation of facts from that of the original contribution, as well as adding important observations and modifications which had since occurred to him.

As he wrote them, the *Three Essays* deal respectively with the sexual aberrations, with infantile sexuality and with the transformations of puberty, in that order. Later he was to introduce his readers to infantile sexuality first and from that to develop the rest of the relevant ideas. This is certainly the more logical and satisfying way to encounter the theory, although his reasons for adopting the original order are easy to understand in the light of his necessity to confront people first with facts from which they could not escape, however much they might deplore them, and only after this with the explanation of those facts in the light of his discoveries.

We can still learn a great deal from studying his own words in those contexts where his final lucidity and conciseness cannot be bettered. An example is his *Introduction to the Development of Sexual Function* in Chapter III of the *Outline of Psychoanalysis,* one of the last works he was ever to write (1939):

According to the prevailing view, human sexual life consists essentially in an endeavour to bring one's own genitals into contact with those of someone of the opposite sex. With this are associated, as accessory phenomena and introductory acts, kissing this extraneous body, looking at it and touching it. This endeavour is supposed to make its appearance at puberty – that is, at the age of sexual maturity – and to serve the purposes of reproduction. Nevertheless, certain facts have always been known which do not fit into the narrow framework of this view. (1) It is a remarkable fact that there are people who are only attracted by individuals of their own sex and by their genitals. (2) It is equally remarkable that there are people whose desires behave exactly like sexual ones but who at the same time entirely disregard the sexual organs or their normal use; people of this kind are known as 'perverts'. (3) And lastly it is a striking thing that some children (who are on that account regarded as degenerate) take a very early interest in their genitals and show signs of excitation in them.

It may well be believed that psychoanalysis provoked astonishment and denials when, partly on the basis of these three neglected facts, it contradicted all the popular opinions on sexuality. Its principal findings are as follows:

(*a*) Sexual life does not begin only at puberty, but starts with plain manifestations soon after birth.

(*b*) It is necessary to distinguish sharply between the concepts of 'sexual' and 'genital'. The former is the wider concept and includes many activities that have nothing to do with the genitals.

(*c*) Sexual life includes the function of obtaining pleasure from zones of the body – a function which is subsequently brought into the service of reproduction. The two functions often fail to coincide completely.

The chief interest is naturally focused on the first of these assertions, the most unexpected of all. It has been found that in early childhood there are signs of bodily activity to which only an ancient prejudice could deny the name of sexual and which are linked to psychical phenomena that we come across later in adult erotic life – such as fixation to particular objects, jealousy, and so on. It is further found, however, that these phenomena which emerge in early childhood form part of an ordered course of development, that they pass through a regular process of increase, reaching a climax towards the end of the fifth year, after which there follows a lull. During this lull progress is at a standstill and much is unlearnt and there is much recession. After the end of this period of latency, as it is called, sexual life advances once more with puberty; we might say that it has a second efflorescence. And here we come upon the fact that the onset of sexual life is diphasic, that it occurs in two waves – something that is unknown except in man and evidently has an important bearing on hominization. It is not a matter of indifference that the events of this early period, except for a few residues, fall a victim to *infantile amnesia*. Our views on the aetiology of the neuroses and our technique of analytic therapy are derived from these conceptions; and our tracing of the developmental processes in this early period has also provided evidence for yet other conclusions.

The first organ to emerge as an erotogenic zone and to make libidinal demands on the mind is, from the time of birth onwards, the mouth. To begin with, all psychical activity is concentrated on providing satisfaction for the needs of that zone. Primarily, of course, this satisfaction serves the purpose of self-preservation by means of nourishment; but physiology should not be confused with psychology. The baby's obstinate persistence in sucking gives evidence at an early stage of a need for satisfaction which, though it originates from and is instigated by the taking of nourishment, nevertheless strives to obtain pleasure independently of nourishment and for that reason may and should be termed *sexual*.[49]

Given this start, we can begin to grasp the whole of Freud's sexual theory. Even while sucking for pleasure is still part of his activities, the baby's gums are hardening and his teeth are on the way. He gains an increase in pleasure and even a sense of power by biting as well as sucking, as many nursing mothers can verify from their own experience. When he is at the breast, his tiny fierceness in chewing on the nipple and his resistance to having it removed from him will produce pain which is not without its pleasurable and exciting aspects to the woman who is suckling him; a determined aggressiveness still markedly noticeable even when she is feeding him on the bottle.

With the further development of the child's consciousness of himself another area becomes charged with pleasurable emotion and capable of being used in two opposite, but equally significant, ways. This is the area of the anus, and particularly the junction of the skin and the ano-rectal mucous membrane. Physiologists have since acknowledged that all junctions of skin and mucous membrane of the body are not only particularly sensitive but are capable on gentle stimulation of producing feelings of pleasure. It is questionable how readily or rapidly this recognition would have been made if Freud had not first directed attention to what he called the erogenous or erotogenic zones, all of which have this feature in common.

Anal pleasure comes first from the physical satisfaction of emptying the bowels, and the secondary reward is the mental satisfaction that the child feels from performing this function for the parents. Nursery language reflects this way of regarding defaecation, often called, for example, 'Doing the big job,' and so on. Here once again power and independence can conflict with the wish simply to please and to gain and bask passively in love. Holding on to the contents of the rectum, obstinately refusing to do one's job in the pot, are ways of defying parental authority. There is an additional pleasure in the actual sensation of retaining the contents of a full rectum, a physical pleasure which is linked to the deferring, and therefore the prolonging, of the opposite pleasure of emptying the bowel.

Overlapping the emergence of both these possibilities of pleasure, with their contradictory means of expression, is the third and final physical pleasure of infancy, that which resides in the genital areas of the body themselves. These, while not yet in any way ready for the full physiological performance of the sexual act, are nevertheless powerful and important areas of pleasurable sensation. At first Freud thought that their stimulation must usually involve an element of deliberate seduction on the part of parents or other children; but his final theory took account of the fact that seduction phantasies were more often than not screen memories from infancy.

In fact, both the normal tendency of the infant to explore his or her own body and such accidental sensations as being dried after a bath, being powdered and even feeling the movement of air on the genital regions, as when a child is naked before or after the bath, can alert attention to the capacity of these areas to provide a special and intensely keen physical sensation of pleasure.

Moreover, Freud was able to link the development of this discovery both with the actual events of infancy and with the symbolism of dreams and adult experience, which we have already encountered. Natural occasions of nakedness, movement through the air, muscular exertion and play, particularly that involving romping and wrestling between children, could all arouse sexual excitement, although of course this sexual excitement would not be recognized as having anything to do with reproduction, or indeed with anything which might become more fully understood and important in adult life.

Indeed, as Freud repeatedly pointed out, it is all too frequently the fate of children to experience innocent sexual excitement during the first five years of life only at the risk of furious adult reprimand, and sometimes of adult threats, proceeding from the repressed infancy of that same adult and recreating the latent fears of rejection, deprivation and mutilation which children inevitably experience from adults who adopt this attitude towards them. The little boy who has discovered that his penis is a source of pleasure is not only liable, but all too likely, to be told by a mother or father who discovers him handling himself, 'If you don't leave that alone, I'll cut it off. . . .' Such threats, sometimes projected by parents on to the family doctor or even the plumber, who will be called in to do the job, are part of the occupational hazard of being a child and discovering one's own physical pleasures and ways of producing them.

In this way, and for this reason, the child's feelings on the subject of his relationship with his parents, and their attitude towards his body and its future, may become deeply divided.

Freud believed that since the child's first intimate human relationship is normally with the mother, or someone who fulfils her role in his nursing and upbringing, she will always be the child's first love. He coined two phrases to define exactly what he meant about this aspect of the development of sexuality in the human race. Sexual objects or love objects are the people or things to whom we direct the libido, our internal drive towards sexual gratification. The channelling of this drive he called sexual aim. Throughout his writings he used the German word '*trieb*', normally translated in the English version of his work as 'instinct', but which could perhaps better be more directly rendered by the word 'drive', or the composite word 'instinctual drive'. The sexual aim is the goal-seeking aspect of the instinctual drive of sexuality; the sexual object, the goal which is sought.

But even in infancy the secret passion of the child for the mother cannot remain either innocent in the child's own mind or capable of fulfilment with any degree of completeness. It cannot be fulfilled because the child cannot have the mother entirely to himself; it cannot remain innocent because the child links the obvious parental disapproval of his sexual excitement with his own secret feelings of jealousy and competitiveness towards his father, whom he inevitably and intuitively perceives as a rival for the mother's affection, attention and all else which he wants from her, and which she is in some way able to give also to his father.

To this situation Freud gave the name of the *Oedipus complex*, based upon the classic Greek myth of the innocent prince of Thebes who the oracle predicts will murder his father and marry his mother. His father has him abandoned, with his feet pierced, on a hillside, to die of exposure and starvation. The child is found and brought up by strangers, finally returning unknowing and unknown, to fulfil the prophecy. Not until he has slain the king, freed the kingdom from the oppression of a wild and terrible creature (the Theban Sphinx), and taken the queen, who is in fact his mother, in marriage, does he become aware of what he has done. In remorse for this inexpiable crime, for which it is evident from the story itself that he has no personal responsibility, he gouges out his own eyes and once again wanders, blind and exiled, through the world.

The Oedipus complex has to be conceived as the child's real but repressed fear that the father will castrate him in retaliation for the desire for exclusive possession of the mother. In attempting to describe this complex in words, we are of course using the words in a way in which no subject of such a complex ever could. No infant could formulate the Oedipus complex in words, nor indeed could an infant confide, explain, confess or even request reassurance in words. Yet feelings as deeply charged as these cannot be endured consciously and so are repressed. With the repression of the Oedipus complex, the period of infantile sexual activity and conscious excitement comes to an end. Sexual feelings remain, but they are diminished and all too often disowned. Curiosity persists, but there are very few children who dare ask questions. The period between about five and about eleven, during which this deceptive calm appears to reign, was called by Freud the latency period.

But the Oedipus complex itself, although the crucial factor in early childhood, is not all which is repressed. Apart from the possibility of the parental threat, why should the child fear castration, and why should the adult carry this fear over to repeat it to the children of the next generation? Freud postulated two answers to this question: one an innate awareness of castration as the ultimate physical violence short of actual murder; the other drawn directly from the child's own experience and observation of his world. Little boys, said Freud, not only discover that their penis is a source of pleasure but they assume that everyone is made as they are, particularly that women and girls have penises as well as men and boys. This certainty survives the earliest discovery that in fact it is not true. Children can have screen memories of seeing women and girls with penises even if they have actually seen them as they really are. But once the idea of castration has occurred, then women and girls provide the awful example of what it must be like. Little girls, on the other hand, discover quite early that they have a clitoris which is admittedly smaller, but in every way similar, to the penis which they see on little boys. For some of them this may indicate an inferiority on their part which they find it hard to escape throughout their lives.

Throughout the whole of the first period of infantile sexual activity, that is from birth until around the age of four or five, both boys and girls possess an equal capacity for seeking and finding gratification, and both make equal use of it. The most obvious but most developmentally advanced method is by infantile masturbation of the genital organs themselves. We have already seen that in little boys this is naturally something they learnt to do by touching or stroking their penis, and in little girls the same attention centres upon the clitoris. But from Freud's theory of erotogenic zones, it is clear that we should be able to discover comparable activity relating to the mouth and lips, and to the anus and ano-rectal junction of skin and mucous membrane. The classical example of stimulation of an erotogenic zone in the mouth is thumb sucking. Freud used this to exemplify infantile sexual activity at its most simple and primitive. He was able to quote the case of a girl who continued this right through childhood, into and after puberty, and who remarked later that even though kissing produced much the same type of sensation, none but the very best of kisses could compete with the satisfaction to be obtained from sucking her own thumb.

Here is libidinal fixation occurring at a level of activity normally important to the child only during early life. Even after this is outgrown and more mature development has taken place, a reversal to this earlier level, which Freud called regression, is liable to take place under conditions of adversity or stress. Moreover in some cases the fixation is relatively absolute, so that further emotional and psycho-sexual development beyond this stage become impossible. This concept of the available quantity of original sexual energy (libido) being limited, and of its compulsive fixation at various levels of development short of maturity in some individuals, was to provide Freud with the basis of his general theory of the neuroses.

Between oral pleasures and genital pleasures come the pleasures of anal excitation or conservation in infancy. We have already seen that expelling or retaining faeces can have both physical and emotional importance to the child, through the sensations of his own body and the relationship with his parents, with which these functions become involved. They can also have a symbolic importance which lasts through life. Faeces are first regarded as a part of himself, and therefore not only a gift but a precious gift, because given from within his own being. But he soon learns that to take an interest in this product, to handle, smell, smear or even touch it, is intensely disapproved by his parents.

Few children have not made this experiment and suffered this experience. In this case the outcome is that faeces then become abhorrent. They are regarded as filthy and unclean, and at a conscious level this is what they symbolize. At an unconscious level, however, they still retain an element of their original value. And where fixation at an anal level has occurred, even though faeces themselves cannot be hoarded indefinitely since constipation cannot last for ever, everything else of value that the individual may acquire may be hoarded and even thereby prevented from achieving its proper use.

The miser who hoards money, the collector who buys valuable pictures, but once he has acquired them neither displays nor looks at them, the obsessive individuals who are compelled to dwell long and unproductively upon uncompleted tasks, are all examples of this kind of symbolic fixation transformed into an overall pattern of activity in later life.

We are now beginning to see how Freud traced the earliest experiences and activities of childhood into the emotions and behaviour of adult life, building the most important cornerstone of this concept into the structure of infantile sexuality and childhood, adolescent, and adult sexual development.

When Freud was asked how he could possibly know that any of these developments took place in infancy, particularly since he himself had acknowledged the power of repression at this stage, his answer was that, with sufficient skill and patience, analysis of an adult would inevitably go back, beyond even the obvious precipitant trauma of any current neurosis or symptomatic act or problem, to the ultimately repressed infantile roots.

There the nature of infantile sexuality was consistently discovered and there, it was reasonable to assume in the light of this consistency, it operated in everybody. Also operative, and discoverable through later analysis, were other comparable complexes such as sibling rivalry, and a dim but significant awareness of the nature of the adult sexual act itself. This awareness is gained from rumours, whispers or, in some cases, the actual witness of adults engaging in coitus, an observation less unlikely than often supposed, if only because adults insist upon believing that such occasions are without meaning to small children. In fact children are intensely disturbed, aroused and excited by overt adult sexuality, imagining coitus as aggression, conquest and helpless abandoned surrender. Appalled and fascinated, they long to participate while fearing desperately to be discovered watching. Years after the first denunciation of this theory Freud was to receive what he regarded as its final confirmation in the first analysis of a child under the age of five, the famous case of little Hans (see page 141).

Another inescapable consequence of the enforced solitary nature of most infantile sexual activity is that practically all expression of it has to take place by some form of self-stimulation, or auto-erotism, which is the underlying feature of masturbation in whatever form it is practised. Whether the infant sucks his thumb, experiences gratifications through the use of his anal sphincter or, having discovered penis or clitoris, gives pride of place to that form of pleasurable excitement, for most of the time the individual has to secure this alone and for himself. Freud took account of the fact that nursemaids, mothers and even fathers might be seducers of children, in the sense of stimulating their infantile sexuality, whether innocently or deliberately.

That this happens is undeniable. Nursemaids have fondled the genital organs of their charges, mothers have caressed their sons and daughters sexually as well as maternally, fathers have excited their sons and daughters by flinging them into the air and catching them, by rocking them in their arms, or by letting them sit astride their legs and having the rhythmic and exciting experience of riding astride the father's knee, which both the child and father enjoy for reasons which neither of them may be able fully to acknowledge. But precisely because most of these acts are both natural and often unrecognized, they are not only innocent but, for the most part, they merely further arouse a pattern of sexual feeling and a channelling of sexual aim, already developing innately in the child. What determines maturation is not only the course which the sexual aim takes but the object to which it is attached. This leads us to a consideration of the sexual perversions.

These can be understood in terms of Freud's theory of sexuality by regarding them simply as deviations of the normal sexual aim, or fixations upon a sexual object short of that normally achieved in adult life, namely a mature member of the opposite sex. Every perversion admits of an explanation in these terms and, because every perversion is to this extent latent in normal infantile sexuality, Freud once described the sexuality of infants as polymorphously perverse. This was an unfortunate choice of words for a man who had already met more than his fair share of opposition. What he meant was that sexuality in infants is innocent, ignorant and undifferentiated; and therefore capable of an infinite variety of partial or incomplete fulfilments. Representation of such incomplete fulfilment at an adult level characterizes all perversions, but once again Freud had the courage to point out that the sexual life of normal adults nearly always exceeds in one direction or another what is conventionally regarded as normal, and this excess, however acceptable between the people concerned, takes its origin from the earlier and multiple undifferentiated activities of childhood. Examples will make this clear.

Probably the commonest form of deviation in adult sexual life is homosexuality, now usually called inversion (an inturning of libido on to an object like oneself), rather than perversion (a turning away from normal heterosexual desire to a desire for partial or distorted symbolic objects). This simply represents a fixation of the libido upon a sexual object not fully differentiated from the individual concerned. Some of its roots extend back to infancy, when children shared the belief that all sexes were made alike and at the same time identified their strongest needs with their mother, whether they were boys or girls. A later accentuation of what we shall see can be regarded as the normal homosexual phase of adolescence can make this point of development the farthest reached by the individual, in which case full expression of sexual feeling can come only through some kind of union and emotional involvement with a member of the same sex.

Perversions are forms of incomplete maturity of sexual object and aim, which prevent full union of any kind with another individual. Among them may be included voyeurism, where looking at other people of the same or opposite sex naked, watching others having sexual intercourse, seeking to see the genitalia of others, or watching them in the act of urination or defaecation, takes the place of a more complete sexual aim. Exhibitionism, the desire to display and if possible to provoke a counter-display of the sexual organs, is the mirror image of voyeurism. Frequently both these conditions exist in the same person, and both are far more common in men than women, because the symbolic aspects of sexuality are more uninhibitedly present in men than in women. Freud regarded women as more sexually inhibited than men in every respect, but this is perhaps one of the ways in which his own personal experience and complex-determined thinking maintained a permanent blind spot in his life (see pages 160 *et seq.*).

Sadism and masochism provide another pair of complementary opposites. Sadism is that aspect of sexuality which demands infliction of pain or humiliation or, in its less severe forms, simply the establishment of physical or emotional mastery over the partner before complete satisfaction can be obtained. Masochism is the opposite tendency: the need to be made helpless, subjected to pain or humiliation, or simply physically overcome for full satisfaction to be felt. Extreme cases of either sadism or masochism can lead to infliction of actual physical injury or submission to repellent physical and emotional humiliation, on the part of those involved. Sexual murders and the abject subjugation which some men will pay prostitutes to inflict upon them in lieu of sexual intercourse are extreme examples of this kind of thing.

Bestiality and pederasty, the desire to seek sexual intercourse with animals or to confine sexual activity to the seduction of children, are other examples of perversion in which the sexual object is grossly abnormal, the most extreme example of an abnormal sexual object which still retains the human form being necrophilia, the capacity or desire to have intercourse only with a corpse. Finally there are those perversions in which some part of one's own or another person's body, or some article of clothing or symbol of this kind, for example stiletto-heeled shoes, furry garments or wisps of silk or nylon, take the place of a human relationship altogether; those are called fetishism, the name being derived from the worship by primitive tribes of inanimate objects believed to contain the essence of a god. Fetishism combines in one act incomplete development of sexual aim and an abnormal selection of sexual object.

In mentioning these things in his *Introductory Lectures* Freud breaks off, almost as though he were responding to the revulsion displayed by his audience, with the expression: 'But enough of this kind of horror!'[50] In fact, however, these horrors become less horrible, in the sense of being more comprehensible, if we do what he asks and apply the fruits of the theory of infantile sexuality to their understanding.

Obviously, homosexuality is simply substitution of the nearer and more attainable goal of a companion of one's own sex for the final challenge of making it with a member of the opposite sex. For men, women carry the threat of an unknown sexual area: an area without a penis, an area from which in infantile phantasy a penis may have been torn out. From this arise the phantasies of damage to the penis by the vulva and vagina of a woman in intercourse. The concept of the vagina which bites off the penis, the vagina dentata, can sometimes be found underlying the preference of a male homosexual for another man.

In woman the threat is more obvious, although perhaps more easily acceptable because more easily recognized and therefore capable of discussion, at least in adolescence. Sexual intercourse with a man, as a normal sexual object, is the outcome of the normal female sexual aim; but this nevertheless involves penetration of her inmost being, the most secret and intimate part of her body, by what not only appears to be but is often spoken of as a weapon, a tool, a prick, an instrument which carries a threat as well as a promise. There is no comparable awareness of danger at the infantile level of interest, in which the daughter identifies with her father, pretends that she herself has a penis and is unthreatened by and can take care of another woman better than a man. The way in which phantasy suppresses and sometimes substitutes for reality is here clearly illustrated. Adult sexual fulfilment, a mature sexual aim with a mature sexual object, depends upon acceptance that ultimately a penis is incomplete without a vulva and vagina; and a woman's desire for a penis is certain to obtain satisfaction once she can accept the sexual role of a man in her life. But phantasies of self-sufficiency or fears of mutilation can drive people to deny either that women have no penis or that a man's penis can be safe within a woman. Here the earliest threat carried over from infancy to adult life can produce the homosexual, through the normal stage of homosexual interest in adolescence itself.

Voyeurism and exhibitionism are even simpler to understand. Prancing about naked is self-evidently satisfying and exciting for children. The antics which young children perform before getting into the bath, the mixture of coyness and self-assertion, the running away and being caught and brought back – the general gaiety and exuberance of this situation are evident to any parent with the capacity for calm, untroubled observation and an open mind. To see and to be seen are important parts of the emotional fulfilment and sexual excitation of children. They are not only not wrong, they are right: for they are at least a step along the way, and they will induce fixation at that stage only if further development is refused, denied, or repressed.

Sadism and masochism underwent an interesting reversal in priority in Freud's thought. At the time of his original *Three Essays on Sexuality* (1905) Freud saw sadism as an extension of the normal aggressiveness and physical and emotional dominance necessary for one partner to secure full sexual union with another. In human beings he regarded this as an essentially male characteristic, although remarking that in some members of the animal species this trait was exhibited by the female. Sexual activity and sexual passivity corresponded repectively to sadism and masochism and, in humans, to normal male and female characteristics. He also observed, not without regret, that the desire and the capacity to achieve mastery and to inflict pain, as evidence of power over others, appeared earlier in human childhood than the limiting emotion of compassion. He expected, and found himself proved right, that both sadism and masochism would always be present in some degree in any one person who showed evidence of either. An abnormal preponderance of one or the other argued also an

abnormal capacity for an interest in the opposite. All this part
of his theory he was able to retain, but later when he evolved
his hypothesis on the life and the death instincts (see pages 156
et seq.) he gave masochism pride of place as the most primitive
source of the two, since masochism embodied the urge to destruction of oneself, the submission to fate, which by this time
he conceived as part of the organic and emotional equipment of
all living creatures.

Fetishism was in some ways the most interesting and illuminating example of all. The developing sexual aim was conceived as being frustrated short of fulfilment at a crucial period
in infancy and, therefore, settling for a *symbol of the possibility*
of such fulfilment, instead of the complete sexual object as
embodied in another person. The normal hazards of adolescent
exploration, experiment, and disappointment, could be imagined as throwing the individual back, through regression,
to the partial and incomplete symbolic substitute for full
maturation, after which the aim would be directed entirely to
the achievement of that object and the libido would be fixated,
perhaps irreversibly, upon the symbol, rather than upon what
it symbolized. Once again, all possible permutations and combinations of fetishism may be seen in clinical practice, and
Freud had encountered most of them: men who could achieve
orgasm with women only if the women wore a certain garment
such as a particular type of shoe, scarf or piece of under-
clothing, men who could achieve orgasm only if they used such
a garment with which to masturbate, or men for whom ultimate sexual satisfaction could be obtained only by dressing in
articles of clothing belonging to, or commonly worn by,
women whom they might otherwise have sought to pursue,
and who might in the end achieve orgasm only by mastur-
bating in front of a mirror, naked except for their fetish symbol
which they wore or clasped to themselves.

Transvestism, the compulsion to wear the clothes of the
opposite sex and to assume privately or publicly the identity of

such a person, is sometimes a neurotic combination of fetishism and inversion, sometimes a psychotic illness in which the
conviction of a reversal of sexual identity demands the fulfilment of every symbolic act which will reinforce this conviction
in external reality, as far as the patient can conceive and
experience it.

Freud had spent a long time in coming to these views, and
had come to them most reluctantly. Even in the first edition of
The Interpretation of Dreams (1900), there is a curious passage
towards the end of Chapter 3 (Standard Edition No. 4, p. 130),
in which Freud remarks: 'We think highly of the happiness of
childhood because it is still innocent of sexual desires.'[51] A corrective footnote was added to this passage in 1911. Later in the
book he writes quite unambiguously of the existence of sexual
wishes even in normal children. In the course of prefaces to
various editions of his *Three Essays*, he nailed his colours
firmly to the mast.

None, however, but physicians who practise psychoanalysis can
have any access whatever to this sphere of knowledge or any
possibility of forming a judgement that is uninfluenced by their
own dislikes and prejudices. If mankind had been able to learn
from a direct observation of children, these three essays could
have remained unwritten.[52]

By contrast with the resistance encountered in presenting
his theories of infantile sexuality and the psychogenesis of
perversions to professional and, later, to lay audiences, Freud's
observations on the transformations of puberty which formed
the third of his essays in this collection were relatively un-
exceptionable even to his most biased critics.

At puberty the latent period ends. Because of the biochemical and glandular changes taking place in the human
body at this time, there is an immense resurgence of all the
sexual drive which characterized infancy, now charged with
the opportunity of fulfilment. The Oedipal conflict, between

desire for exclusive possession of the mother, and therefore jealousy of the father, and the opposing feelings of fear of her rejection, ultimate punishment by the father and an underlying respect and love for him, all of which combined to produce the repression responsible for the latency period, is now resurrected. The comparable conflict in girls, whereby they make a special play for the father once their complete dependence on the mother has begun to yield to a recognition of the father's role and interest in them, earlier repressed, now also emerges. Following the pattern of naming fundamental conflicts after Greek tragedies, the daughter's temporary fixation upon her father is sometimes called the Electra complex.

The outward effect of these changes is that the adolescent boy becomes rebellious and challenging to parental authority, often particularly to that of his father, while treating his mother with what often seems to be an uneasy mixture of private affection and public assertion, oscillating between dependence and an attempt to dominate. He shows this by leaving her more things to wash, expecting her to do more for him and, at the same time, refusing to recognize the responsibilities of a grown man in the family in terms of the father's leadership and organization. A girl at the same age will defy her mother but openly seek to win over her father by flagrant displays of feminine attraction, about which she can at first seem naïve and shameless, but which later reveal themselves as experimental trials of her femininity for its final aim in seeking a mate outside the family. The stages of adolescence recapitulate to some extent the stages of infancy with their oral, anal and genital preoccupations, but genital primacy is reached relatively early and other aspects of infancy reappear in a disguised form.

Narcissism, the preoccupation with oneself as an object of love, is to some extent a normal phenomenon during adolescence. Boys begin to concern themselves with their appearance as much as girls do; it is at this stage of their lives that both sexes begin to be particularly vulnerable to appeals to their vanity or threats to their private phantasy of what they wish to be like. Creams and ointments are employed for clearing the complexion in both sexes, or for increasing the size or the contour of the breasts in girls. In both sexes proclaiming a defiant sexuality by hair style and clothing becomes an important aspect of adolescent life. It is not difficult to understand how this period of narcissism leads into a period of normal homosexual interest when the drive for the love object outside the individual's own self becomes more powerful. The first and most immediate object outside oneself is someone like oneself. Moreover, as we saw earlier (pages 99, 100), the challenge inseparable from maturation is less if the first involvement with another person is with someone not totally unfamiliar, someone unconnected with repressed infantile phantasies of what the other sex may be like.

As Freud pointed out towards the end of his essay on the *Transformations of Puberty*, the barrier against incest is a mysterious one.

We have said that the parents' affection for their child may awaken his sexual instinct prematurely (i.e. before the somatic conditions of puberty are present) to such a degree that the mental excitation breaks through in an unmistakable fashion to the genital system. If, on the other hand, they are fortunate enough to avoid this, then their affection can perform its task of directing the child in his choice of a sexual object when he reaches maturity. No doubt the simplest course for the child would be to choose as his sexual objects the same persons whom, since his childhood, he has loved with what may be described as damped-down libido. But, by the postponing of sexual maturation, time has been gained in which the child can erect, among other restraints on sexuality, the barrier against incest, and can thus take up into himself the moral precepts which expressly exclude from his object-choice, as being blood-relations, the persons whom he has loved in his childhood. Respect for this barrier is essentially a cultural demand made by society. . . . One of the tasks implicit in object-choice is that it should find its way to the opposite sex. This, as we know, is not accomplished without a certain amount of fumbling. Often enough the first impulses after puberty go astray, though without any permanent harm resulting. Dessoir (1894) has justly remarked upon the regularity with which adolescent boys and girls form sentimental friendships with others of their own sex. No doubt the strongest force working against a permanent inversion of the sexual object is the attraction which the opposing sexual characters exercise upon one another. Nothing can be said within the framework of the present discussion to throw light upon it.[53]

Freud pointed out that the tendency for adolescent and young adult love to show a regressive pattern could result in every degree of arrest or fixation of libidinal development, from a total absence of normally conscious sexual desire, through a tendency to fall in love with thinly disguised parent-figures of the opposite sex, up to that marginal immaturity of personality consistent with an arrest of psychosexual development in the later stages of adolescence.

These last are limited only in so far that their demands for love exceed their capacity for giving it, and particularly their capacity for giving it in terms of an adult sexual relationship, by the same margin which could be expected in a child, but which can be fatal to marriage and stability in adult society.

Freud also took the opportunity of this essay to restate the essential concept of 'libido'. This is a relatively fixed quantity of energy in every individual, related primarily and essentially to their sexual drive, part of the equipment with which they are born, and enduring, in whatever form it finds expression, throughout their life into their old age. Libido can become fixed at various levels as we have already seen.

Once he had conceived the idea that it could be treated almost as though it were a physical quantum of energy, Freud also constructed a hypothetical framework whereby it could be attached in varying quantities to different objects and complexes. He called this attachment 'cathexis', and spoke of libido being cathected to whatever the object or complex might be. The greater the cathexis in any one direction, the smaller the free and available quota of libido left at the disposal of the individual. The earlier and more complete the fixation, the less chance the individual would have to attain sexual maturity, and indeed the less drive he would experience towards that end.

Almost all the phenomena of Freud's theoretical interpretation of conscious and unconscious psychological existence have now been reviewed. There remains only consideration of the formal structure which completed his concept of the design of psychic life, and the application of completed theory to an understanding of neuroses. The immediately subsequent chapters will deal with both these matters, completing them with briefly illustrative case studies.

Finally the wider impact of his theories, as he was later to elaborate them, and some of the most important modifications which he introduced will prepare us for the conclusion of the book, in which we shall have to review the outcome of what Freud really said and its continuing reverberations throughout the life and thought of the human race.

6 The Concept of Psychical Structure and Function

One of the most interesting books which Freud ever wrote was also one of the shortest and one of the last. We have already quoted from it: it is called *An Outline of Psychoanalysis* and was published in English in 1939. What is chiefly remarkable about it is the extreme conciseness and definition of its language. There was also a note of austerity about it, as though the author knew well that he was reaching the end of his span of human life and no longer needed to justify or persuade his readers of the truth of what he said. That part of his work was finished. Others would follow, would develop, criticize or modify it. But this final and brief report upon experience supplies some of the most crisp statements of his formulated theories that are to be found anywhere. He wrote an introductory note to it, as follows:

The aim of this brief work is to bring together the tenets of psychoanalysis and to state them, as it were, dogmatically – in the most concise form and in the most unequivocal terms. Its intention is naturally not to compel belief or to arouse conviction.

The teachings of psychoanalysis are based on an incalculable number of observations and experiences, and only someone who has repeated those observations on himself and on others is in a position to arrive at a judgement of his own upon it.[54]

The first two chapters were devoted to what Freud called the 'physical apparatus' and the 'theory of the instincts'. In our own explorations, they are all that remain to make the accumulated body of knowledge which is psychoanalysis complete for our purpose. We can then see its applications, first in the understanding and the treatment of illness, then in the wider world towards which Freud was ultimately to direct it. For the concluding sections of the first part of this book we can turn for a while to direct quotation from Freud himself. No one can say what he said in this context better than he said it himself.

The Psychical Apparatus

Psychoanalysis makes a basic assumption, the discussion of which is reserved to philosophical thought but the justification for which lies in its results. We know two kinds of things about what we call our psyche (or mental life): firstly, its bodily organ and scene of action, the brain (or nervous system) and, on the other hand, our acts of consciousness, which are immediate data and cannot be further explained by any sort of description. Everything that lies between is unknown to us, and the data do not include any direct relation between these two terminal points of our knowledge. If it existed, it would at the most afford an exact localization of the processes of consciousness and would give us no help towards understanding them.

Our two hypotheses start out from these ends or beginnings of our knowledge. The first is concerned with localization. We assume that mental life is the function of an apparatus to which we ascribe the characteristics of being extended in space and of being made up of several portions – which we imagine, that is, as resembling a telescope or microscope or something of the kind. Notwithstanding some earlier attempts in the same direction, the consistent working-out of a conception such as this is a scientific novelty.

We have arrived at our knowledge of this psychical apparatus by studying the individual development of human beings. To the oldest of these psychical provinces or agencies we give the name of *id*. It contains everything that is inherited, that is present at birth, that is laid down in the constitution – above all, therefore, the instincts, which originate from the somatic organization and which find a first psychical expression here (in the id) in forms unknown to us.

Under the influence of the real external world around us, one portion of the id has undergone a special development. From what was originally a cortical layer, equipped with the organs for receiving stimuli and with arrangements for acting as a protective shield against stimuli, a special organization has arisen which henceforward acts as an intermediary between the id and the external world. To this region of our mind we have given the name of *ego*.

Here are the principal characteristics of the ego. In consequence of the pre-established connection between sense perception and muscular action, the ego has voluntary movement at its command. It has the task of self-preservation. As regards *external* events, it performs that task by becoming aware of stimuli, by storing up experiences about them (in the memory), by avoiding excessively strong stimuli (through flight), by dealing with moderate stimuli (through adaptation) and finally by learning to bring about expedient changes in the external world to its own advantage (through activity). As regards *internal* events, in relation to the id, it performs that task by gaining control over the demands of the instincts, by deciding whether they are to be allowed satisfaction, by postponing that satisfaction to times and circumstances favourable in the external world or by suppressing their excitations entirely. It is guided in its activity by consideration of the tensions produced by stimuli, whether these tensions are present in it or introduced into it. The raising of these tensions is in general felt as *unpleasure* and their lowering as *pleasure*. It is probable, however, that what is felt as pleasure or unpleasure is not the *absolute* height of this tension but something in the rhythm of the changes in it. The ego strives after pleasure and seeks to avoid unpleasure. An increase in unpleasure that is expected and foreseen is met by a *signal of anxiety*; the occasion of such an increase, whether it threatens from without or within, is known as a *danger*. From time to time the ego gives up its connection with the external world and withdraws into the state of sleep, in which it makes far-reaching changes in its organization. It is to be inferred from the state of sleep that this organization consists in a particular distribution of mental energy.

The long period of childhood, during which the growing

human being lives in dependence on his parents, leaves behind it as a precipitate the formation in his ego of a special agency in which this parental influence is prolonged. It has received the name of *super-ego*. In so far as this super-ego is differentiated from the ego or is opposed to it, it constitutes a third power which the ego must take into account.

An action by the ego is as it should be if it satisfies simultaneously the demands of the id, of the super-ego and of reality – that is to say, if it is able to reconcile their demands with one another. The details of the relation between the ego and the super-ego become completely intelligible when they are traced back to the child's attitude to its parents. This parental influence of course includes in its operation not only the personalities of the actual parents but also the family, racial and national traditions handed on through them, as well as the demands of the immediate social milieu which they represent. In the same way, the super-ego, in the course of an individual's development, receives contributions from later successors and substitutes of his parents, such as teachers and models in public life of admired social ideals. It will be observed that, for all their fundamental difference, the id and the super-ego have one thing in common: they both represent the influences of the past – the id the influence of heredity, the super-ego the influence, essentially, of what is taken over from other people – whereas the ego is principally determined by the individual's own experience, that is by accidental and contemporary events. . . .

The Theory of the Instincts

The power of the id expresses the true purpose of the individual organism's life. This consists in the satisfaction of its innate needs. No such purpose as that of keeping itself alive or of protecting itself from dangers by means of anxiety can be attributed to the id. That is the task of the ego, whose business it also is to discover the most favourable and least perilous method of obtaining satisfaction, taking the external world into account. The super-ego may bring fresh needs to the fore, but its main function remains the limitation of satisfactions.

The forces which we assume to exist behind the tensions caused by the needs of the id are called *instincts*. They represent the somatic demands upon the mind. Though they are the ultimate cause of all activity, they are of a conservative nature; the state, whatever it may be, which an organism has reached gives rise to a tendency to re-establish that state so soon as it has been abandoned. It is thus possible to distinguish an indeterminate number of instincts, and in common practice this is in fact done. For us, however, the important question arises whether it may not be possible to trace all these numerous instincts back to a few basic ones. We have found that instincts can change their aim (by displacement) and also that they can replace one another – the energy of one instinct passing over to another. This latter process is still insufficiently understood. After long hesitancies and vacillations we have decided to assume the existence of only two basic instincts, *Eros* and the *destructive instinct*. . . .[55]

In this last sentence Freud is referring to the outcome of one of his final and most controversial modifications of the established theory of psychoanalysis, published as a monograph with the title of *Beyond the Pleasure Principle* in 1920. Before encountering this further, we can summarize our total knowledge of the psychoanalytic hypothesis with all the rest of the relevant data before us.

Freud regarded consciousness as only a relatively small and transient part of the total mental life of an individual. We can share his recognition of it as an immediate, constantly changing reflection of everything of which we are aware at a given instant in time; the range of this awareness being limited by our human capacity and its raw material coming from two separate but equally important sources, the first the sum total of sensory information which we are receiving from the outside world, and the second the impact of everything which at that instant in time we may be remembering from the past. The more our attention is devoted to past memories, the less will we be aware of present changes in our environment; and although the reverse is often apparently true, in that in the heat of the moment and the press of action we may forget things which otherwise we would have remembered, we have also learned that even the most acute external stimulus may gain an added significance in consciousness by its immediate association with something remembered from the past.

If consciousness is then the sum total of everything of which we are aware, pre-consciousness is the reservoir of everything we can remember, all that is accessible to voluntary recall: the storehouse of memory. This leaves the unconscious area of mental life to contain all the more primitive drives and impulses influencing our actions without our necessarily ever becoming fully aware of them, together with every important constellation of ideas or memories with a strong emotional charge, which have at one time been present in consciousness but have since been repressed so that they are no longer available to it, even through introspection or attempts at memory.

These three definitions do Freud's views justice, but they are not exhaustive. The id is entirely and necessarily unconscious: the ego is that part of it which has been separated to establish contact with the external world and has also thereby found itself able to receive information from within the body and the mind, as though it were observing. But it remains a part of what it observes and, just as it is free neither of the impact of the external world on the one hand, nor of products of the id and of repressed complexes on the other, so too it is influenced by a super-ego, that aspect of childhood acceptance and respect for adult authority, standards and ideals which has eventually been introjected. 'Introjected' was Freud's own word; it means taken once again into the self, at an unconscious level. There established, the super-ego exerts its own separate and often opposing influence, to mediate between the ego, which is the awareness of self, the ego's experiences of the external world and its challenges, and the ego's experiences of the impulses of the id and its instinctual drives.

The analogy of the iceberg has sometimes been used to remind us that the unconscious area of mental life is vastly greater than the conscious or consciously remembered areas. If everything that we know and remember is regarded as the part of the iceberg above the surface, at least seven times as much lies below the surface, and determines both the centre of gravity of the whole, and much of the movements, direction and fate of the iceberg.

Another way of visualizing the relationship between consciousness, pre-consciousness and the unconscious mental life is to regard the whole area as a vast darkened arena containing innumerable potential memories, ideas and experiences.

Consciousness is the spotlight which, sweeping the arena, lights up just that area upon which it falls. Everything outside its illumination, but within its range, is preconsciousness. In this analogy the manipulation of the spotlight can be imagined as the responsibility of the ego, but the mechanism is powered by the id and governed by the super-ego, and the ego can move it only with their aid. Whatever the outcome of these forces, there will always be areas of the arena beyond the range of the spotlight altogether: these can never normally be illuminated and so are unconscious. Sleep, dreams, hypnosis and free association widen and extend the spotlight's range, but may distort or diffuse its illumination. Not for nothing has psychoanalysis been called a voyage into the unknown, an exploration of the darkness.

For some time Freud sought to relate his discoveries to neurophysiological activities within the brain but here success eluded him, and eludes us still. However, he was able to point to a relationship between the associative method of recall and the network of nerve filaments and electrical circuits within the brain on which this must depend and which provide innumerable links between one idea and another. Much of this had been known and studied for many years before his time; but once again it was his particular contribution to point out the vitally important role played by emotion in determining whether or not a chain of associations would in fact be readily followed, and could lead automatically to a particular idea or constellation of ideas appearing in consciousness.

Similarly, he was aware of the biochemical nature of nervous and glandular activity. He gave it full weight not simply in the chemistry of sexuality and adolescence, but also in his remark that one day perhaps the psychoses and possibly even the neuroses might be susceptible of changes brought about by biochemical means, rather than by the admittedly cumbrous and exhaustive method of psychoanalysis. But until that day came he believed that he and his disciples had to work with the most effective tools at hand. And for Freud the most effective of all was the application of psychoanalysis.

*The General Theory of
the Neuroses*

Freud's theory of sexuality and of the maturation, potential for fixation and capacity for regression of libidinal energy has already shown its relevance to disturbances of sexual maturation and personality. What follows in this chapter is the overall theory of the neuroses, as finally presented by Freud. The ideas are taken from every stage in his writings on this subject, the earliest from those emerging from *Studies on Hysteria*, right up to the final pieces of general exposition in *The New Introductory Lectures on Psychoanalysis*, in 1933.

From an early state in his encounter with the neuroses, Freud had shown a remarkable readiness to accept them as basically real and very crippling forms of illness. This *was* remarkable, because in his day the entire range of clinical phenomena represented by neurotic illness was apt to be swept under the medical rug and either stamped on or, as far as possible, forgotten. Patients whose symptoms, although couched in terms of physical complaint or mental anguish, could not be demonstrated to be due to some tangible structural cause, were regarded simply as sand clogging the fine cogs of the medical machine. They were considered degenerates, in so far as they were permitted to have a cause of any kind allotted to their overall disability. Yet they formed, as they have always formed, not less than fifteen per cent of the total sum of human suffering in the world; and the mechanisms which underlay their suffering contributed to at least another fifteen to twenty per cent of all illness of every kind.

Before seeing how Freud classified and sought to understand neuroses, a simple definition, with some illustrative examples of the kind which he himself was prepared to give frequently, repeatedly and at length, will help to prepare the reader to recognize Freud's particular contribution to this field.

Neuroses are now recognized as disorders of the pattern of thought, feeling and behaviour which develop during the life of the individual, and tend progressively to limit and disable that individual's capacity for normal existence. They may take a number of forms, but in general their effect is to produce cumulative disaster in the individual's personal and social life; in work, play, confidence and what passes for courage and success in the everyday world. It was possible in Freud's day, and it is possible now, to take simple clinical examples for the main forms of neuroses. We can list them and then consider them briefly one by one:

(1) Hysterical illnesses and hysterical personality.

(2) States of anxiety and anxious and vulnerable personalities.

(3) Obsessive compulsive disorders and obsessional personalities.

(4) Neurotic depression and personalities specifically vulnerable to defeat and despair of this kind.

(5) Hypersensitive, suspicious and paranoid attitudes, and the personalities prone to them.

(6) Specific disorders of sexual immaturity, and personalities involved in and damaged by this.

This is not a text-book list, nor is it an exhaustive list of neurotic disorder. Marginal degrees of emotional immaturity and vulnerable, immature or explosively infantile personalities, sometimes called psychopathic personalities, can also be included; and beyond the whole range of neuroses and neurotic personalities there are what are called the psychoses. These are disorders of experience of which the cardinal clinical feature is a disruption of the individual's contact with, and capacity for normal interpretation of, his external environment and of experiences reaching him from within his own body.

Freud wrote frequently of the relationship between psycho-analysis and psychiatry, although in his day this relationship was charged with an antagonism unmerited by either side. Nevertheless, apart from regret and occasional retaliation, for example by reference to the undoubted ignorance of dynamic psychology and analytical principles displayed by the great majority of psychiatrists, Freud himself clearly recognized the limitations of psychoanalysis as a clinical and therapeutic technique in psychiatry, particularly where the psychoses were concerned.

Of the list of neurotic disorders set out above, we have already encountered hysteria in the opening part of this book. It was a starting point for Freud's investigations, and will only be exemplified here by a simple clinical illustration. A previously healthy young adult, woman more often than man, may develop symptoms of loss or disturbance of sensation generally, of motor power, of memory, of special sensations such as vision or hearing, to the extent that she is quite dis-abled by this. These symptoms are accompanied frequently by a more child-like dependence, and at the same time a more child-like demand for magical relief, than would normally be consistent with such a patient's age and intelligence. Every-one in the environment, and particularly those closest to the patient, becomes involved in this, and reacts usually with a mixture of anxiety, resentment, and a concern often projected on to the doctors, of whom either a denial of the reality of the symptoms, or alternatively a miraculous cure, is classically demanded. These are the patients whom Freud met, treated, learned from and described in his writings, up to the time when his clinical practice began to expand to include the whole area of neurosis in its province.

States of anxiety and anxious, vulnerable people are likely to be encountered both earlier and more frequently than hysterical reactions or personalities. But Freud discovered them only after encountering the release of such anxiety following disturbance of that pathological equilibrium which hysteria or hysterical symptoms had achieved. Common examples include people who are generally apprehensive, constantly in a state of fear of whose origin they can give no account, or who develop specific fears, which they know to be absurd, in relation to quite trivial and ordinary everyday events, such as going out by themselves or remaining alone in the house, travelling in public transport or sitting other than in the aisle seat in the theatre. Such patients also suffer characteristic disturbances of physiological equilibrium including increased heart rate, respiration and blood pressure; and disturbances of digestive capacity and sleep rhythm.

Long-standing anxiety will lead to depression, and in many people states of depression may occur in response to what might seem otherwise normal and expected stress. Bereavement classically produces depression, and Freud linked these two states in a brilliant monograph entitled *Mourning and Melancholia*. But combinations of loss of zest, of hope, of capacity for joy or pleasure, physical or sexual appetite and, again, disturbances of digestion or sleep rhythm, together with loss of weight and general debility and exhaustion, tended to be ignored or misdiagnosed, largely because their recognition as illnesses in their own right proved embarrassing in the absence of any effective treatment for them.

Meticulous individuals are common in any community. Those whose meticulousness has reached obsessional proportions, so that they are not free to lead normal lives nor to sustain normal social relationships because of their preoccupation with cleanliness, with the necessity for everything to be done in a certain way or with rigid codes of conduct for themselves and for others which make life extremely difficult for all concerned, are also as numerous today as they were when Freud first encountered them. The essential symptoms of obsessive compulsive illnesses consist in apparently meaningless and aggravating rituals which have to be undertaken, either in the

patient's mind or in actual physical performance in the course
of his or her day-to-day life.

The necessity to count up to certain numbers or to repeat
certain stereotyped phrases, originally of a reassuring or en-
couraging kind, can make a patient's life miserable. These
may be linked to the necessity to perform exasperating and
repetitive rituals such as checking the gas taps or electricity
switches a routine number of times, and then by multiples of
that number until the process is never-ending – the necessity
to wash before, during and after the performance of every
domestic task in the house and then to involve clothes, walls or
entire rooms in these ritual cleansing operations – in the conviction that otherwise some terrible form of damage, infection
or contamination will follow. Such are the symptoms which
can drive such a patient to eventual despair, and rapidly exhaust
the patience of everyone concerned with them.

Suspicious, sensitive and paranoid attitudes can be illustrated by people who believe that others are gossiping about
them, denigrating them, or ready to conspire against them in
even the most trivial and unlikely fashion. In such ways
otherwise well-intentioned and kind-hearted housewives can
feel excluded from the local social circle, from the church group
or wives' fellowship, can refuse their children permission to
join the Boy Scouts or the Girl Guides or youth clubs, because
of a groundless conviction that they are despised and rejected
by their neighbours. This kind of misery is often linked with
pathological jealousy, and suggests a psychotic severance from
reality more often than a purely neurotic development. But
Freud was able to throw considerable light on its mechanism
and give comparable understanding as to how it should be
handled.

The sixth group, sexual perversions, has already received
illustration in the chapter on the theory of sexuality; and so,
with this picture of the clinical material which confronted
Freud now in our minds, we can turn to his own remarkably

succinct and comprehensive theory of the psychogenesis of all
these conditions.

The theory starts with Freud's recognition that instinctual drives were fundamental in shaping the course of an
individual's life. By far the most important is the sexual
instinctual drive, or libido, present from the first dawning
consciousness of the infant until the last fluttering breath of
the dying adult. In Freud's view, all life depended on libidinal
development, except to the extent that he later modified his
theory to include the death instinct, which we have yet to encounter. The libido can be compared to crude oil gushing
from the centre of the earth, capable of refinement and transformation into innumerable end products, giving the essential
drive and source of energy to every human activity. By the
way in which it is channelled and developed, the libido carves
the structure of the personality, just as a river carves the structure of its own banks in finding its course from the mountains
to the sea. Freud maintained that frustration of the libidinal
drive was the cause of anxiety; although the most primitive
of all forms of anxiety he ascribed to the individual's experience
of the normal process of human birth.

We believe that in the case of the affect of anxiety we know what
the early impression is which it repeats. We believe that it is in
the act of birth that there comes about the combination of un-
pleasurable feelings, impulses of discharge and bodily sensations which has become the prototype of the effects of a mortal
danger and has ever since been repeated by us as the state of
anxiety. The immense increase of stimulation owing to the
interruption of the renovation of the blood (internal respiration)
was at the time the cause of the experience of anxiety; the first
anxiety was thus a toxic one. The name '*Angst*' – '*Angustiae*',
'*Enge*' – emphasizes the characteristic of restriction in breathing
which was then present as a consequence of the real situation and
is now almost invariably reinstated in the affect. We shall also

recognize it as highly relevant that this first state of anxiety arose out of separation from the mother. It is, of course, our conviction that the disposition to repeat the first state of anxiety has been so thoroughly incorporated into the organism through a countless series of generations that a single individual cannot escape the affect of anxiety even if, like the legendary Macduff, he 'was from his mother's womb untimely ripped' and has therefore not himself experienced the act of birth.[56]

Anxiety is therefore inescapable in Freud's view, indeed there can be no human being who has not in fact experienced it, albeit in situations in which they would regard the external or internal threats or dangers to be sufficient reason for its appearance.

Anxiety is the commonest form of distress from which we can suffer. But anxiety is something more; it is a situation which, prolonged, produces disturbances of physiology and of mental equilibrium which can become intolerably destructive. Nevertheless, Freud believed that the sources of anxiety, together with the feelings aroused by them, could be repressed and the entire constellation of feelings and experience could be banished from consciousness and pre-consciousness into the unconscious area of the mind. It was their partial, distorted or disguised re-emergence under pressure which produced the symptoms of hysteria: a conversion from repressed anxiety to overt but quite changed experience of loss or distortion of function. In this concept both anxiety and hysteria are linked and, indeed, for Freud the occurrence of a mixed syndrome called 'anxiety hysteria' was a definite clinical entity. Even where complete repression did not take place, he believed that libido could be arrested by the *threat of frustration* or the *denial of fulfilment* in young children and, even more, by the *denial that such fulfilment could reasonably be desired or acknowledged*. It is in the final failure of communication, rather than in the failure of complete fulfilment, that the most serious damming up of libido is believed to occur. Such damming up produces fixation at a level short of completeness, or regression to a level less likely to involve threat and misery. These mechanisms, acting in varying degree, provide the dynamic explanation of the neuroses in Freud's general theory. We can now examine it in its final and crystallized form.

Freud classified the neuroses in terms of their aetiology: that is, of their causation. His classification divided them first into actual neuroses and psychoneuroses. Actual neuroses were disturbances of subjective well-being and physiological balance, entirely consequent upon a frustration of libidinal fulfilment or exhaustion of libidinal energy. He saw them as the outcome either of a complete inhibition of sexual activity of any kind at every stage of the individual's life, or due to an exhaustion of sexual energy by, for example, excessive masturbation. Direct anxiety was the expression of dammed-up sexual energy; direct exhaustion, in the form of irritable fatigue or neurasthenia, was the effect of over-expenditure of such energy. For neither of these conditions did Freud consider psychoanalysis appropriate.

They were experiences of distress entirely due to faulty patterns of activity and did not necessarily represent the intervention of any unconscious mechanism. If such patients could not be relieved either of frustration on the one hand or of exhaustion on the other, both of which were presumably susceptible to relief by an alteration in their pattern of life and relationship with others, then they would not get better. If, on the other hand, they *could* be relieved of these two pathological patterns then the symptoms would clear up. Understandably, Freud regarded both these types of neuroses as relatively uninteresting, and they tended to drop out of his writings in the later years.

What *is* interesting is that they were probably both total misconceptions. They may well provide one of the few examples of hypotheses, advanced by the supreme exponent of unconscious mental mechanisms, which both ignore the activity of the unconscious and are based upon precisely that kind of crude oversimplification which Freud himself was to detect, with devastating accuracy, in the formulations of other and less enlightened colleagues. As a subdivision of the neuroses in general, 'actual' neuroses probably do not exist. These conditions which were regarded as falling under this heading were probably either anxiety states on the one hand, or states of mixed anxiety and depression on the other.

The second group, the psychoneuroses, were to provide the heart and core of Freud's clinical interest and discovery. These were patterns of neurotic activity entirely determined by unconscious mechanisms, in response to the various hazards to which the unconscious drive towards unconditional libidinal satisfaction must inevitably expose the developing human being. Freud divided the psychoneuroses again into two groups, the transference neuroses and the narcissistic neuroses. The transference neuroses were essentially treatable by psychoanalysis and, indeed, provided the main indication for its use as a therapeutic technique. The narcissistic neuroses defied such treatment, for reasons which become apparent when they are studied, but which had the effect of excluding them from the practical range of psychoanalytic treatment altogether.

Anxiety neuroses, anxiety hysteria, hysterical conversion neuroses and obsessive compulsive neuroses were transference neuroses. Severe neurotic depression, paranoid states and those borderline states of disturbance which lay between personality disorder and schizophrenia were narcissistic neuroses. They are readily separated, and the mechanisms can be easily stated, in the light of the knowledge we have already shared about Freud's theories in respect of them.

Anything which threatens, denies or absolutely prohibits the fulfilment of libidinal satisfaction can set up a state of anxiety. External events can do this, but so also can the inhibitory functions of the super-ego. If we can see no way out, or if our conscience or our unconscious judgement denies that there is a way out or forward or prohibits its use, then we can be overwhelmed with anxiety. Our response to this anxiety may be to regress to a state where our demands are less and therefore our relative achievement relatively unthreatened; or it may be to distort our attempts so that they take forms which are converted into symptoms, while some of the anxiety still persists. Symptoms of hysteria and anxiety co-existing are of course the basis of anxiety hysteria as Freud conceived it.

Hysterical symptoms are conversions of otherwise completely repressed anxiety and all that produced it in a threatening situation, and hysterical personalities are those whose level of total emotional maturity and integration leave them no possibility of fulfilment, except through such converted or distorted expression. Underlying the whole of this dynamic pattern, Freud saw as decisive the Oedipus complex – the threat to the infant of its inevitable desire for exclusive possession of the mother, with the inescapably concomitant risk of talion punishment from the father. Either this remained a source of unmitigated threat, always productive of anxiety and constantly repeated throughout life, or else the growing child learnt to recognize that while mother must remain finally unattainable she was, of course, not irreplaceable; an adult love object must, indeed, take her place in terms of sexual maturity; and while father remained understandably important he was neither omnipotent, nor inevitably threatening.

Moreover, the father too could share his pattern of authority with others, so that the final acceptance of authority in communal life became an adult recognition of the need for stability in society and no longer an unconscious fear of castration or annihilation, as a penalty for any kind of criticism or contrary aspiration. Success in the resolution of Oedipus complex was in fact Freud's prescription for the avoidance of neurosis; resolution of the complex the key to its treatment. Failure to resolve the Oedipus complex was the reason for the development and the maintenance of the neurotic state.

Recalling what Freud said about the psychoanalytic procedure, and tracing, with him, the resistances inevitably encountered within it back to unconscious mechanisms within the patient thereafter projected upon the analyst, we can see why he called these neuroses 'transference neuroses'. The failure to resolve the Oedipus complex could only be finally reversed in psychoanalysis if the patient could transfer to the analyst all the products of that unresolved complex, with its hate, love, grief, pain, disappointment, shame and lingering flicker of expectation, and then work them through in such a way that ultimately the analyst ceased to be father, mother, brother, lover and almost divine saviour, and to resume his place as a doctor who had done a job.

By this point the patient would have grown up. The part of the analyst was therefore that of a catalyst in a complex chemical process: a component which enabled the resolution and completion of the process to be achieved, but which emerged at the end as uninvolved as it had been before the process started, although at every stage in the process its influence was necessary to enable that process to go through.

Freud postulated therefore three essential stages in successful analysis of a transference neurosis. The first stage was the establishment of a transference, and the evocation and elucidation of all the material repressed because no solution had been possible. The second stage was the re-emergence of the original neurotic emotional pattern, but this time cathected by the transference to the analyst, with whom were relived all the unresolved conflicts with or about parents or others in the patient's childhood, conflicts which still dominated the patient's relationship to the rest of the world. Since this relationship was a neurotic one, the transference relationship was in itself a second neurosis, taking the place of the first. With the resolution of the transference neurosis the patient could achieve maturity and the analyst could retire from the scene, with the patient's recognition and appreciation of what had been done, but no longer with the complications of the intense feelings, projections and regressive attachments which were part of the transference, and from which the patient could only be freed by the analyst entering into and thereby resolving this turbulent stage of his life.

Freud considered that the third group of transference neuroses, the obsessional or obsessive compulsive neuroses, were the most exemplarily characteristic of all. These are his own words about obsessional neuroses, taken from his *Introductory Lectures*:

Obsessional neurosis is shown in the patient's being occupied with thoughts in which he is in fact not interested, in his being aware of impulses in himself which appear very strange to him and in his being led to actions the performance of which give him no enjoyment, but which it is quite impossible for him to omit. The thoughts (obsessions) may be senseless in themselves, or merely a matter of indifference to the subject; often they are completely silly, and invariably they are the starting-point of a strenuous mental activity, which exhausts the patient and to which he only surrenders himself most unwillingly. He is obliged against his will to brood and speculate as though it were a question of his most important vital problems. The impulses which the patient is aware of in himself may also make a childish and senseless impression; but as a rule they have a content of the most frightful kind, tempting him, for instance, to commit serious crimes, so that he not merely disavows them as alien to himself, but flies from them in horror and protects himself from carrying them out by prohibitions, renunciations and restrictions upon his freedom. At the same time, these impulses never – literally never – force their way through to performance; the outcome lies always in victory for the flight and the precautions. What the patient actually carries out – his so-called obsessional actions – are very harmless and certainly trivial things, for the most part repetitions or ceremonial elaborations of the activities of ordinary life. But these necessary activities (such as going to bed, washing, dressing or going for a walk) become extremely tedious and almost insoluble tasks. In different forms and cases of obsessional neurosis the pathological ideas, impulses and actions are not combined in equal proportions; it is the rule, rather, that one or other of these factors dominates the picture and gives its name to the illness, but the common element in all these forms is sufficiently unmistakable. Certainly this is a crazy illness. The most extravagant psychiatric imagination would not, I think, have succeeded in constructing anything like it; and if one did not see it before one every day one would never bring oneself to believe in it. Do not suppose, however, that you will help the patient in the least by calling on him to take a new line, to cease to occupy himself with such foolish thoughts and to do something sensible instead of his childish pranks. He would like to do so himself, for he is completely clear in his head, shares your opinion of his obsessional symptoms and even puts it forward to you spontaneously. Only he cannot help himself. What is carried into action in an obsessional neurosis is sustained by an energy to which we probably know nothing comparable in normal mental life. There is one thing he can do: he can make displacements, and exchanges, he can replace one foolish idea by another somewhat milder, he can proceed from one precaution or prohibition to another, instead of one ceremonial he can perform another. He can displace the obsession but not remove it. . . .[57]

This gives us a clue as to the nature of obsessional neurosis as Freud illuminated it. It is a displacement neurosis. Freud saw obsessional neurosis as essentially a regression of the libido to the earlier infantile stage of sadistic-anal organization; a stage in which the infant could not directly experience, even in imagination, the possibility of a love for the parents free from aggressive, destructive and defiant impulses. This aggression transforms normal relationships into deeply unconscious infantile ones. For the idea 'I would like to love you, and to enjoy you in love', there exists in the repressed form only the idea 'I should like to be strong enough to kill you'. This latter idea contains the phantasies of omnipotence which are the infant's compensation for his developing awareness of his helplessness in relation to those whom he wants to love. The regression has also affected the range of libidinal direction, the sexual object, as well as the sexual aim. The impulses which are conflicting, and against which such tremendous unconscious resistance has to be mobilized, apply essentially to those who are nearest and dearest to the patient; and so the obsessional rituals are displaced, but highly emotionally charged, defensive actions designed to propitiate or prevent the fear that he himself may damage, destroy, contaminate, or in some way become sexually involved in a forbidden way with the person whose very identity must be concealed from him and who is, in fact, his father or his mother or both.

Freud made it clear that in his view precisely the same mechanisms of displacement, over-valuation, condensation, regressive symbolism and distortion with which we are already familiar through our study of his *Interpretation of Dreams* and unconscious processes in general, were operating in obsessional neuroses as in sexual perversions. The essential difference between the sexual perversion and the obsessional neurosis was simply that in the latter, repression, the final denial and banishment into unconsciousness of the sexual nature of the whole procedure, was achieved. But, here again, obsessive compulsive neuroses qualified for inclusion in the general group of transference neuroses because, by establishing and then working through a transference, both the regressive and the repressed aspects of the distortion could be reversed and the patient could eventually emerge with the capacity for a mature love object, that is, the capacity to love another human being of comparable age and opposite sex; while the analyst, released from the intense and contradictory bonds of transference, could once again fade painlessly from the scene.

Nevertheless, experience was to teach Freud that the analysis of an obsessional neurosis could often be excessively difficult and prodigiously long. The patient was apt to use precisely the same mechanisms of regressive symbolization, distortion and a compulsive doubt about the meaning of even the simplest words and interpretations, to maintain unconscious resistance. Resistance in anxiety states, in anxiety hysteria and in hysteria itself was primarily emotional or purely inhibitory. The patient either objected to, became indignant about, or simply could not remember, what was relevant to the analysis.

But in the obsessive compulsive neuroses a more subtle and sometimes finally irreducible mechanism was at work. The fundamental rule of analysis was turned into its most powerful opponent. Confronted with the task of saying everything that came into his mind, the obsessive patient would begin by producing an interminable amount of largely irrelevant material, pausing to criticize, doubt, sift and inquire about the meaning of every aspect of it so that the symbolization of words or feelings became an entrenched mechanism, and analysis, which ultimately depended upon the use of words for the communication of feelings, could be held indefinitely at bay.

One of Freud's later pupils, Fenichel, brilliantly illustrated this difficulty by an analogy. He compared the task of successful analysis in an obsessional patient to that of someone who tries to dry a companion, who has just fallen into the river, with the towel which that companion was clutching at the time of his immersion. The instrument of analysis is ultimately verbal communication, upon which the transference of emotion depends.

If, as has already happened in the ritual symbolization of conceptual thought in such conditions, the very process of analysis itself is meaninglessly dissected and analysed by the patient instead of the underlying feeling being allowed to emerge, then the whole process can become sterile and defeated. It is upon the establishment of a transference, the enduring and working through of a transference neurosis and its final resolution that the therapeutic success of psychoanalysis ultimately and always must depend.

This prepares us for the discovery of the limitations of psychoanalysis in the face of what Freud calls the narcissistic neuroses. In these disorders the libido has been withdrawn from the outside world altogether. In the technical jargon which we cannot always avoid if we are to remember the words which Freud actually used, the object cathexis of normal developing emotional life is lacking. The essential characteristic of psychotic illnesses, of the more severe forms of depression, paranoid delusions, delusions of grandeur, of persecution and of the excessive self-concern with which these conditions are characterized, is that, in them, the libidinal cathexis of objects has been withdrawn. When one asks what has happened to the libido of these patients, the answer is that it has been turned in and back upon the ego itself, and that this turning back is the source and essence of the illness. Because of this, there is no possibility for the analyst to elicit the necessary degree of rapport with the patient for the patient to form a transference, and to turn this transference into a plastic substitute for the illness itself, with which the analyst can work and from which the analyst can free the patient. Patients with narcissistic neuroses are simply not interested in analysis or even in the analyst himself. They live in their inner world of woe or exaltation, of terror or despair, and have nothing to offer or to accept from the outside world.

This single statement explained for Freud the inability of psychoanalysis to deal effectively with the analysis of severe depression, of paranoid delusions, of schizophrenia and even of certain states of extreme regressive and narcissistic self-concern which might be present as hysterical illnesses or disorders of personality, but which in fact prevented a terminable analysis. In one of his last papers on technique, *Analysis Terminable and Interminable*, Freud reopened this subject at some length. By this time (1937) most of his disciples had

finally accepted his own view, based on his and their experience, that psychotic states and those states of severe depression or exaltation, in which the patient was for long periods
apparently inaccessible to pure communication, were totally
resistant to and indeed sometimes simply exacerbated by
psychoanalysis.

But even so, there were still many attempts to employ
psychoanalysis as the sole treatment for such conditions in
hospitals where psychoanalysis had finally won support and
enthusiasm. Even when the time-wasting futility of this
procedure had been recognized in most enlightened psychiatric centres, there remained pupils and followers of Freud
who insisted upon believing that all transference neuroses, at
least, must certainly be susceptible of treatment by psychoanalysis and that psychoanalysis was the only and universally
indicated treatment for such cases. The object of *Analysis
Terminable and Interminable* was the sound of a warning blast
on the prophetic trumpet by the originator of psychoanalysis
himself, to prevent blind and uncritical devotion from becoming itself regressive and destructive.

Some patients have suffered a withdrawal of object cathexis,
an inhibition of the further development of libido, a regressive pattern of its reinvestment in themselves and a fixation at
this level of such magnitude that successful analysis is not only
impossible, but the attempt to undertake it simply reopens the
patient's unfulfilled longings for a total all-embracing dependent relationship with another human being who will be everything to him: mother, father, brother and child; and so the final
effect is to produce an indissoluble transference neurosis of
malignant proportions.

When this had happened in Freud's own practice the treatment had been broken off either by him, by the patient or by
the patient's relatives. He gives instances of this in his writings,
but again seems not to recognize that this is only a more complicated repetition of the original headlong flight from the

transference situation undertaken by Breuer; a flight which led to Breuer's parting from Freud and losing his friendship, after the case which had been crucial in this respect.

In his later years, Freud was progressively to limit the therapeutic indications of psychoanalysis. But he remained convinced that even when it could not cure its use would always illuminate the unconscious mechanisms at work in the production of psychogenic symptoms, and thereby enrich the total of human understanding of illness in which this played a significant part.

Reviewing this aspect of the general theory of neurosis, and its application, from the relative distance of another twenty-five years, with all the advances in the physiological and biochemical treatment of psychotic illnesses which this last twenty-five years have brought, it is easier to see now what Freud was never fully to express or finally to acknowledge: *namely, that what he called the narcissistic neuroses are probably not primarily psychogenic in origin.* It remains true that their psychodynamic components could not be understood without an awareness of psychoanalytic principles. But they themselves correspond more to what Freud had called 'actual' neuroses than to transference neuroses – their origin being glandular and biochemical rather than emotionally mechanistic.

Exceptions are always possible: for example states of mourning and depression which outlast in intensity and duration anything which natural grief could explain, or states of excessive vulnerability, defensiveness, hypersensitivity and suspicion arising from an awareness of a total incapacity to meet the emotional demands of everyday adult life. But in general what they have in common is that psychoanalysis is useless in their treatment, by contrast with physiological techniques; and relatively sterile in their understanding, by comparison with biochemical researches. Schizophrenia, in those days still most frequently called dementia praecox, and the overwhelming depressive illnesses with delusions of absolute worthlessness and decay certainly owe a great deal of their intensity to chemical and physiological factors. They are in this sense comparable to states of delirium, the outcome of changes in the neurophysiology and biochemistry of the brain and central nervous system, produced by disorders of metabolism or intercurrent disease, which fragment or distort the entire psychic life to the point at which communication of the kind required for psychoanalysis becomes totally impossible.

Dazed, bludgeoned, bewildered and bemused by the disturbance of normal consciousness proceeding from this disorder of metabolism and central nervous function, the patients may well react with symptoms which can be analytically interpreted. But in fact these are the outcome of, rather than the cause of, their disability. In schizophrenia the egg is the biochemical disturbance, the chicken the emergent illness with its pathetic, poignant combination of malevolent despair, incongruity and contradictory mixtures of elation, terror, dream and delusion. It would be impossible to analyse a schizophrenic patient to complete recovery unless the underlying physiological disturbance had subsided or been reversed.

Freud returned to a consideration of the differences between neuroses and psychoses in clinical psychiatry and the way in which these differences might be related to his own theories of the structure of the personality and its dynamic development. In a short paper called *Neurosis and Psychosis* he hit upon what he believed to be the decisive formula.

Transference neuroses correspond to a conflict between the ego and the id; the libidinal drive reaching the ego from the id has been frustrated, distorted, subject to inhibition or aggression, or fixated at a level short of fulfilment, because the circumstances of the ego could not completely express or tolerate it. Then narcissistic neuroses remained those in which the withdrawal of libidinal attachments or cathexis to the outside world left an overwhelming reinvestment of emotion and concern attached to the ego itself. These, therefore, were neuroses in which little or no contact could be made between the patient and the analyst, in terms of the formation of a transference relationship.

Pursuing the special example of melancholia, the depressive illness most resembling mourning, Freud concluded that there the ego is in fact mourning for somebody or something who has been lost or denied and with whom, once all investment of libido in that person or possibility has been withdrawn, the ego now identifies itself. 'I cannot have you any longer for myself, and so I will become you for myself. . . .' But this unconscious mechanism is not enough to prevent the sense of outward loss. Not only must the lost object be abandoned and its image identified with the ego, but the lost object must become a bad object because it has been lost, otherwise its loss would be quite unbearable. It may have to be so bad an object that it no longer deserves to live.

In these circumstances, the ego having taken this object into itself, or introjected it, then becomes victim to the superego which threatens, criticizes or punishes the ego in this situation unmercifully. In this way Freud explained the tremendous denigration and despair which is so characteristic a feature of severe depression. If contact with reality was finally broken, then this despair would be heightened and intensified by delusions, either of punishment to come or of self-destruction which must be inflicted. Suicide in such depressive illness represented the killing of the ego by the self at the command of the super-ego.

Schizophrenic illnesses, chiefly characterized either by a disintegration or by a totally unrealistic and entirely subjective relationship with the outside world, based on phantasy, formed the third group of illnesses. These were psychoses in their own right, and represented either an unwillingness or an incapacity of the ego to relate to the external world, as it really was, any longer. In such a state patients might be unable to communicate or might even fail to recognize the world and the people with whom they lived. Reduced to essentials the formula then ran: transference neuroses correspond to a conflict between ego and id, narcissistic neuroses (of which melancholia is a supreme example) to a conflict between ego and super-ego, and psychoses to a conflict between the ego and the external world.

'It is true,' wrote Freud of this theory, 'that we cannot tell at once whether we have really gained any new knowledge by this or have only enriched our store of formulas. . . .' [58]

And one might expect that, were he to have written this paper in 1964 instead of 1924, he might well have added that the centre of physiological disturbance of brain function, presumed to be operative in both depression and schizophrenia, would certainly have to be taken into account in explaining the narcissism of the former, and the total inability of the ego to relate to the external world in the latter. Seen against the background of this possibility, the psychoanalytical formula is indeed a valuable one. It only loses its value when the attempt is made to substitute it for the biochemical hypothesis, instead of allowing it to take place alongside it.

Freud was able to demonstrate a particularly elegant formula in the case of paranoid schizophrenia, that variety of psychosis in which the individual believes himself to be the object of persecution by other people, who are either entirely non-existent or who, in the reality of the outside world, may have neither knowledge of his existence nor any wish nor motive to persecute him whatsoever. The central theme is a threatening sexual desire, first denied, then displaced, finally repressed, to re-emerge as a distorted rationalization. The dynamics of paranoia then resolve themselves as formula for the defence of the ego against an awareness of homosexuality, which in this case is unacceptable and repressed. The formula

goes as follows: 'I, a man, love him, a man.' But this truth
proves absolutely unacceptable to the ego. Denial follows:
'I do not love him; on the contrary, I hate him.' This remains
beyond acknowledgement, because the amount of aggression
contained in this formula is too much for the ego to bear. The
final displacement projects this feeling upon the other person,
or upon all men: 'It is not that I do not love them, but rather
that they hate and do not love me. It is their hatred for me
which leads them to persecute me. I remain innocent.'

The close relationship between homosexuality and paranoia
was supported in Freud's view by the frequency with which
paranoid delusions took the form of intense pathological
jealousy of other people. A man might become jealous of his
wife because his repressed homosexual impulses compelled him
to deny that he did not want her, and forced him to substitute
the displaced projection that she did not want him and was
therefore being unfaithful to him. As always, the price of compulsively maintained innocence can be delusional.

8 Three Summarized Case Histories

Freud's case histories were unique in clinical psychiatry; they were an even more original step in the history of medicine itself. Never before had the sufferings of human bondage been described in such intimate and yet clinically penetrating terms. Of the dozen or so reported in detail, five are generally regarded as being the most important. Two of these deal with psychotic illnesses; almost certainly, from Freud's own description, varieties of schizophrenia. The remaining three will be briefly recounted here: they are respectively a case of hysteria, a phobic anxiety state and a case of obsessive compulsive neurosis.

The Case of Dora

This was the first case published by Freud after the joint work with Breuer, and had as its full title *Fragment of An Analysis of a Case of Hysteria*. Its original title was *Dreams and Hysteria*, and its purpose was to demonstrate the role played by dreams in the analysis of hysteria. The case history itself centres around two dreams produced by the patient and analysed in detail.

Freud hesitated for some time before publishing this case. He first presented it for publication in 1901, but then withdrew the manuscript and kept it for another four years before he could finally bring himself to allow it to reach the professional audience for whom it was intended.

The original patient in the case of Dora had been her father, whom Freud had treated for syphilis. Four years after his recovery he had brought his daughter to Freud and Freud

accepted her for psychotherapy. At that time the girl had
refused to enter treatment. Two years later, however, she
returned of her own accord, treatment was begun and maintained for three months, after which Dora broke it off and
vanished from Freud's knowledge.

Dora was eighteen years old when treatment began, the
younger of two children, the other of whom was her brother
who was nineteen and a half. The father was in his late forties
and the mother, a year or two younger, was described by Freud
as a woman suffering from so complete a preoccupation with
the details of housekeeping that she had no time for personal
relationships with her family. Dora's symptoms at this time
were varied and manifold; most of them had been present for
many years, some for more than half her life. Freud regarded
them as classical hysterical symptoms; they included reading
difficulties, a nervous cough, loss of voice, sometimes for weeks
at a time, migraine, depression, hysterical aggressiveness followed by withdrawal from social situations, preoccupations
with suicide which would punish her family for their lack of
understanding and a general dissatisfaction with life.

In the course of analysis Freud learnt from Dora that her
father had become involved in an affair with a neighbour's
wife. The neighbour, Mr K., had himself made sexual advances to Dora and had even proposed that he should marry
her if her father divorced her mother and married his wife.
Dora's illness arose out of her love for her father, the conflict
aroused by the proposals of the neighbour and her identification with the neighbour's wife, who was a much warmer figure
than her own mother. All this in turn was tied up with her own
family situation, which basically was classically that of an
Oedipus conflict. However, Freud never got as far as dealing
with this last and, he was later to discover, most crucial phenomenon. Dora remained in treatment for three months, at the
end of which time she broke it off without explanation. Fifteen
months later she returned for one further consultation, saying

that she had made considerable symptomatic improvement although she was still far from completely well.

In the concluding part of his case report, Freud frankly discussed his failure to analyse either the early infantile situation or the transference between Dora and himself, which had undoubtedly played a part, both in her initial improvement and then in her actual rejection of him and his treatment. In retrospect he recognized that such improvement as had taken place was entirely due to an unanalysed transference, and that the chief lessons to be learnt from the case were the accessibility of dynamic material to free association in hysterical patients, and particularly to free association of their dreams, and also the unwisdom of accepting symptomatic improvement, 'the flight into health', as evidence that the neurosis had been cured.

There is an interesting footnote to this case. Many years later, in 1922, Dora consulted another analyst, this time Dr Felix Deutsch, a Viennese consultant and disciple of Freud. After Dora's death, Dr Deutsch published his own experience of this early case. He was able to confirm Freud's interpretation and predictions about the patient, in a number of instances. She had never come to terms with the unresolved Oedipal conflict, or the later repercussions of it caused by what she unconsciously interpreted as the incestuous approaches of Mr K. and her strong identification with his wife, with whom her father was having an affair. She herself remained frigid and disgusted both with marriage and with heterosexual relationships in general. She was an unhappy illustration both of the perceptiveness of Freud's early work and the inconclusiveness of its results in terms of therapy.

The Case of Little Hans

In the light of the general theory of psychoanalysis this case is quite the most astonishing of all Freud's publications. It was published in 1909 as a paper entitled *The Analysis of a Phobia in a five-year-old Boy*. Little Hans was a child who became afraid of going out of doors, giving as his reason the fear that a horse would bite him. His father was a firm believer in Freud and his theories and brought the problem, but not the boy, for Freud's help. Freud advised the father on the treatment of the child, which was carried out almost entirely by proxy, by the father himself, who was of course deeply involved in the child's neurosis. Freud himself saw the boy only once, but seems to have seen nothing remarkable in this at the time, or indeed later, despite its evident contradiction of his own psycho-dynamic theories of the unconscious significance of the Oedipal relationship, which emerged as the basis of the phobia as the child revealed it to his father.

The child told his father his fears and his dreams, asked both father and mother questions and drew pictures for them to illustrate his problem. This had begun when he was three and a half, after the birth of a sister, which had set him thinking about where babies come from, how mummies produced them and what are the roles of a mummy and daddy in this matter. At the same time he displayed considerable interest in and preoccupation with his own penis which he called his 'widdler', and with the penises of other people, particularly his father, developing his interest in horses after noticing that they had singularly large penises.

The horse phobia is described as a direct outcome of all this, and Freud interpreted it to the father in terms of the Oedipus complex: father had a bigger penis than little Hans, and might threaten him if little Hans admitted to his father how much he wanted his mother to himself. Pride of possession would go to the one with the biggest penis, and a horse, with the biggest penis of all, was a subject of displacement whereby Hans' fears of what his father might intend for him were displaced on to horses who would bite him if he went out. The protection which Hans sought was over-determined as in dreams. Not only did he stay in to avoid being bitten by horses: he stayed in with mother instead of going out with father.*

In fact, these parents, although probably a good deal more enlightened than most in the Vienna of the early 1900s, still committed most of the insightless solecisms central to the psychoanalytic hypothesis of adult threats leading to infantile castration complexes. Little Hans' mother told him that if he played with his widdler she would send for the doctor to have it cut off;† little Hans' papa rebuked him for his overt and

* It must be added however that little Hans' horse phobia admits to a somewhat simpler explanation, which is in fact the one the child offered himself before being told repeatedly by his father and by Freud, on the one occasion when they met, that this was 'a lot of nonsense'. The child's own explanation was that he had first become afraid of horses after hearing that horses might bite you, and seeing one of a pair of big horses harnessed to a van fall down and struggle in the street.

This case is worth reading in the original for the parallel development which the narrative shows, between the child's undoubted interest in his own and other people's sexual development and his subsequent fear of horses. But every consequential link assumed to exist between the one and the other is revealed on inspection to be the outcome of an interpretation or an affirmation by Freud or the father, and sometimes indeed simply the unsupported affirmation itself. This has been the subject of a critique by two contemporary writers, Joseph Wolpe and Stanley Rachman. (*The Journal of Nervous and Mental Disease*, Vol. 130, No. 8, August 1960.)

† Excerpt from this conversation as reported by Freud:
Mother: 'If you do that, I shall send for Dr A to cut off your widdler, and then what will you widdle with?'
Hans: 'With my bottom.'
It will be seen that Hans was a resourceful and courageous child. Later this further exchange occurred between mother and son, while Hans was 'looking on intently while his mother undressed'.
Mother: 'What are you staring like that for?'
Hans: 'I was only looking to see if you'd got a widdler, too.'
Mother: 'Of course. Didn't you know that?'
Hans: 'No, I thought you were so big you'd have a widdler like a horse.'[59]
It is usually assumed that in this instance Hans' mother told him

innocently-confessed interest in widdlers, until Freud suggested that this might reasonably be a topic for discussion
between father and son. But even after this father could not
resist arguing with mother and finally dragging the child
away, because he disapproved of her indulgence in letting the
little fellow spend some time in her bed in the mornings.

Despite all these vicissitudes, little Hans recovered completely and was able to accompany first mother then father
out on walks, notwithstanding the horses which they encountered. He was also able to discuss the topic of widdlers to
his satisfaction with his father, after which Freud presumed
that the original fantasy of the doctor's removal of his penis,
implanted in his mind by his mother, had changed for the
better by being altered into a belief that his father approved of
the fact that he and his widdler would grow up and get bigger
in time; although the role of the mother in this preoccupation
was never discussed between them.

Some fourteen years later an elegant young man appeared in
Freud's office and announced, 'I am little Hans.' He had been
well during the whole of this period, had followed his father's
profession which was that of musician, and was embarked
upon a musical career. According to available reports, he has
led a comparatively normal life since that time. Nevertheless,
he was completely without memory of his phobic anxiety
state, of any of the therapeutic discussions with his father, or
of his single visit to Freud. His second visit was a matter of
courtesy since the name Freud had figured largely in the
family.

---

what amounted to a deliberately defensive lie. This is true only if the
assumption is made that they were both talking about the possession
of a penis. If in fact their common language referred to the means of
passing water, they they may have understood each other better than
Freud or Hans' father understood either of them. This possibility is
never mentioned in the case history.

Freud ascribes to this case the single importance that for the first time infantile sexuality had been clearly demonstrated in an infant, rather than being deduced by the retrospective analysis of dreams and memories in adults. Freud remarks that the case held for him nothing that he did not know already: but it did confirm what he had been trying to teach everybody else. Freud himself never displayed any enthusiasm for child analysis, and it is perhaps touching and characteristic that the only case for which he was directly responsible was in fact one in which his active participation was minimal, and the entire therapeutic work was carried out by the central figure in the child's own Oedipus complex, his father.

The Case of the Rat Man

This was reported with the original title of *Notes upon a Case of Obsessional Neurosis*. Freud's main purpose in publishing this case was to illustrate the mechanisms of displacement and sadistic anal eroticism which he felt underlay most cases of obsessional neurosis. The case report makes both its formulation and its foundations very clear.

This case is in fact an account of a complete and successful analysis lasting eleven months. The patient was relieved of his symptoms and, up to the time of his death in World War I, had remained well. The name frequently given to the case is derived from the central obsessional fear that the patient expressed. This was concerned with an appalling torment, which a fellow-officer on manoeuvres with him had mentioned in passing as a form of punishment occasionally used in the East. The victim was tied down, a pot containing rats was turned upside down on his buttocks and the rats were left to gnaw their way out through the victim's anus. The patient had found this idea fantastic, disgusting and yet revoltingly fascinating.

In the course of the manoeuvres during which he had

heard this alarming anecdote, the patient had also lost his spectacles. He had wired to Vienna for another pair from his optician and, in between the loss and the delivery of a new pair, had listened to the story of the rat punishment just recounted. He had immediately conceived the idea that, unless he followed a very complicated programme of actions and thoughts calculated to avert a catastrophe of this kind, this punishment would be visited on the two people most dear to him: his father and the woman he loved. In fact, his father had been dead for some years and he had no reason at all to suppose that the woman he loved was in any danger. This made no difference whatsoever to his obsessional rumination on this subject, and the expiatory actions which he felt compelled to perform.

In the course of Freud's account of his early interviews with this remarkable young man, one is given a vivid impression of the analyst's own sense of bewilderment at the determined, meticulously recounted but entirely confusing inconsequentiality of the programme which the patient contrived for himself. It involved paying a particular officer for the spectacles, which had been delivered to a village a little distance from the headquarters of the manoeuvres, becoming convinced that if he did pay this man the punishment would be visited upon his father and the woman in question, and then becoming equally convinced that this would be their fate if he did not pay the money. Since the latter conviction led him to make a vow that he would pay it and to bind himself to this, it then became decisive.

The early part of the history includes an involved account of the journeys, decisions, counter decisions and indecisions surrounding all his activities; for example, arranging that he should pay the money to the officer whom he believed had paid it on his behalf, then finding that this officer had had nothing whatever to do with the transaction, hoping to take him and another officer who was in charge of postal deliveries for the regiment to the post office, where the first one should pay the money to the young woman there, she should give it to the second who he believed had paid it to her on his behalf in the first place, and that he should repay the first, thereby keeping his vow.

In the course of this narration the reader, Freud and the patient become equally confused. Freud himself remarked that it is impossible completely to disentangle the account as the patient gave it. But even so he becomes involved himself in drawing maps of where the patient allegedly travelled and illustrating what the patient was trying to do; the total impression is one of an obsessional confusion in which all who participate become inextricably involved.

Ultimately, the history becomes one of early infantile sexual implication in the exploration of female genitalia in a governess, doubts about sexual identity and preoccupations surrounding his father, himself and women. Freud observes that the officer clearly felt 'an unconscious horror at the pleasure' which the whole central incident, surrounding his learning of this Eastern torture, provided.

Analysis revealed that he had had obsessional ideas, fears and rituals of various kinds since his childhood, and that the crucial event which brought him to consult Freud was only the culmination of the mounting crescendo of these feelings, finally triggered off to a complete state of horror, confusion and disgust, with enormous intensification of ritual thoughts and actions, after the story told him by his fellow-officer. Throughout the entire course of the analysis there are innumerable examples of the patient's characteristic hesitations and cancellations of his own decisions. For example, on one occasion the woman he loved was due to leave a certain town, and he was walking along the route her carriage would take on the way to the station when he saw a stone in the road. He immediately felt compelled to remove it in case the carriage wheel should run over it and the carriage then overturn and harm her. As soon as he had removed it he was not sure whether he had not put it in a more dangerous position, or that its removal might not cause some other catastrophe. He therefore felt compelled to replace it. Actions of this kind, originating and then cancelling what were intended to be acts of precaution or expiation, were constantly occurring.

Two further instances out of a large number included in the case history can be given: the first concerns the patient's suicidal impulses, which had to be denied by intense mental effort. He told Freud that on one occasion he had lost some weeks of study because the woman whom he loved had gone away to nurse her grandmother who was seriously ill. While he was working hard at his studies in her absence and missing her, the idea had occurred to him:

' If you received a command to take your examination this term at the first possible opportunity, you might manage to obey it. But if you were commanded to cut your throat with a razor, what then?' He had at once become aware that this command had already been given, and was hurrying to the cupboard to fetch his razor when he thought: 'No, it's not so simple as that. You must go and kill the old woman.' [60]

Freud points out that what had happened was that his resentment against the old grandmother for being ill had led him at first to wish for her death, then to imagine that he intended it, and finally to consider himself as fit only to kill himself for entertaining such savage and murderous passions. But in the patient's consciousness these ideas occur in fact in reverse order, and much less clearly.

The second instance concerns the complicated journeys and arrangements centring around the payment for his second pair of spectacles delivered to the post office while he was on manoeuvres. Ultimately he recognized that he had felt interest in the girl at the post office, who would provide a more accessible female companion than the woman whom he loved, who was both distant and capricious from time to time. His earliest

sexual experience had made him both jealous and ardent to
know more of the mysteries of the female body and tempera-
ment, and he had felt cheated and frustrated about this ever
since. His father, inevitably, stood as a symbol of the barrier
between his youth and inexperience and the maturity and confidence which he wished for but could not attain. It was for
this reason that the father was included in the fantastic punishment which his own feeling of guilt made him ruminate about
continually and continually try to prevent.

The entire case history is replete with examples which
could have come from cases of obsessional neurosis seen by
any physician in clinical practice. His earliest preoccupations
with sex he found both pleasurable and agonizing, but productive of continuing anxiety and frustration; while his reaction to experiencing his first erections was to go to his mother
to complain about them. He had wondered whether this was
necessary, since he had already conceived the morbid idea that
his parents knew all his thoughts, an idea which he could
explain to himself only by supposing that he had spoken them
out loud without hearing himself.

These three cases have been selected out of the total of
eleven of the longer case histories published by Freud, because
they illustrate three aspects of the analysis of a transference
neurosis; others clamour for inclusion, but can be read in their
original versions. The most intensely described is the case of
The Wolf Man, so called because of a dream he reported in
which a tree outside his bedroom window was crowded with
wolves, about which he had multiple phobias.

Freud's analysis of this patient's infantile memories provided both patient and physician with a direct recall of the
primal scene: a term coined by Freud to denote witnessing
of the sexual act by a child.

Just before reaching the point at which, with considerable
circumspection, he finally plunges into an account of this

hypothetical visual experience on the part of his patient, aged at that time about eight, he remarks:

I have now reached a point at which I must abandon the support I have hitherto had from the course of the analysis. I am afraid it will also be the point at which the readers' belief will abandon me. . . .[61]

Reading Freud's case histories as a whole, perhaps their most striking features are his remarkable memory for detail and his exhaustive capacity to deal with all the complexities of the case, using them to support the various hypotheses adduced in the presentation. No other analyst has equalled this particular feat, although it is doubtful whether anyone but the founder of psychoanalysis would have been able to make quite such wide use of the meticulous wealth of detail gathered in the histories. One paradoxical result of this is that, despite the vividness and clarity with which he was capable of writing, Freud imposes enormous burdens upon his readers. The temptation to skip or to attempt to systematize case histories is great: the recognition of the tediousness as well as the tremendous labour inherent in the original procedure of psychoanalysis inescapable. Nothing would be gained by quoting further in detail from the Wolf Man or other cases, but once again the reader who wishes to give himself an experience of what might be called the pure essence of Freudian clinical description, inference, deduction and presentation can do no better than turn to the original case history as Freud wrote it and discover for himself whether the anguished cry, uttered by the writer and quoted above, touches his heart and his imagination, or simply echoes his horrified disbelief. Freud would have been prepared for either, and would have forgiven both.

9   *Additions and Revisions
     to the Total Theory*

Throughout his life Freud continually reviewed and revised his theories. Just as he had accustomed himself to making room in his concept of an individual case for any new material which might suddenly emerge and seem to contradict or challenge the formulation he had already reached, so with his theories as a whole he endeavoured to keep them not simply up to date, but capable of offering a reasoned and scientific explanation of the world, as he saw it, and the way in which men and women lived, loved, strove and suffered. In the course of this book we have had to anticipate some of the later discoveries, in so far as to have omitted them when first considering the theories of dreams, of sexuality and of the structure of the personality would have left those theories incomplete.

But, before we move on to the wider implications of psychoanalysis as Freud himself saw it, we have a final task in understanding the basic nature of the work: to review some of the developments for which Freud was himself responsible, but which by no means all his followers have felt able completely to accept or to incorporate in their own work. There have been many analysts since Freud who have made their own additions, subtractions, limitations and extensions of the theory. Here we can be concerned only with the originator himself.

The most important revisions and extensions to be considered concern respectively ego and depth psychology, the psychology of groups, the life and death instincts, some further views on femininity and concepts of sublimation, super-ego and conscience.

The Ego and Depth Psychology

The total personality, as Freud came to regard it, consisted of ego, super-ego and id. Because the ego was caught between the often opposing forces of its two companions in this analogy, but also was the sole member of the three responsible for making the actual adjustments to external reality which normal human life demands, the ego was constantly in a position of extreme vulnerability. Driven by instinctual drives from the id, commanded or forbidden by the super-ego, even its unconscious attempts at resolution of these conflicts subject to censorship and, all the while, in waking hours compelled to deal with the hard, bright, beckoning, but often cruel world in which the individual lived, the ego had constant need of defences. Freud was to return to these, and his daughter, Anna, one of his most famous pupils, wrote a monograph especially devoted to a study of the ego and its mechanisms of defence.

Freud was particularly struck by his growing recognition that while the ego was so vulnerable, and might even have to be divided consciously against itself in so many human situations, it was the only part of the entire psychic structure with which another human being could make contact. The analyst, confronted by a patient clearly deeply divided, contradictory and uncertain about his very willingness to seek or accept help, had yet to find that part of the ego with which he could ally himself, while accepting that another part, dominated by the super-ego or compelled to make unconscious and uneasy compromises between the id and the outside world, might remain his enemy. In addition to repression and the various dream-work mechanisms including displacement, distortion, symbolization and regression, other defences exist. These include flight, as for example the literal flight from physical disaster when people run away from an earthquake – or more subtle flight, from contemplating threatening aspects of their lives, exemplified in the case of Dora by her flight into apparent health as an alternative to continuing an alarming series of personal discoveries in analysis.

We have already encountered projection and introjection as varieties respectively of displacement and identification: melancholia can be their pathological outcome, but falling in love can also be interpreted in similar terms. The loved person becomes the source of all that is most desired in life, so that recognition of that person's real nature may be totally obscured by the helpless determination with which the ego has incorporated the loved one into the lover's own personality. Alternatively, every dream and hope the lover has ever cherished may be projected on to the object of his love. In either case, rational judgement is out of the question. Shakespeare had had the same idea: '. . . Love is merely a madness. And I tell you deserves as well a whip and a dark cell as madmen do.' (*As You Like It: Rosalind in a gay aside to Orlando, in the Forest of Arden.*)[62]

The Psychology of Groups

In his one personal study of group psychology, Freud clarified, perhaps for the first time, the dynamics of the leader principle: a kind of falling in love en masse, whereby groups of people will turn to a leader and hand over their super-ego judgements to him before introjecting his standards into themselves.

The most convincing and terrible example of this principle in action occurred in the unquestioning and uncritical acceptance of the Fuehrer, Adolf Hitler, by the German-speaking people, ultimately including Freud's native Austria.

Freud pointed out two ways in which the idealization of a leader, with the abandonment of even the possibility of criticism, can unite, and therefore give a sense of security and belonging to, a group. It can be done through imposed and accepted discipline, as in an army, or through devotion to a shared idea, as in a religious movement. Obviously these two examples are not mutually exclusive, but the significant difference is what happens when the leader is defeated or overthrown, or abandons his followers. Where the bond has primarily been imposed by discipline, the leaderless group becomes a rabble, less certain or ready to defend themselves or their principles than they might have been had they previously been independent individuals. When the bond has been one based on ideas and the willingly invested emotion which accompanies them, such a group, rendered leaderless, may feel threatened on all sides but will probably turn to hostility towards those outside it, and may well project the loss of the leader on to them. Freud believed that the persecutions carried out by Christianity, both between its own sects and against the Jews, provided appalling examples of this release of hostility in an otherwise ostensibly peaceful and humble organization, supposedly ruled by the idea of universal love. We shall be further concerned with this aspect of his views in the penultimate chapter of this book.

Application of the complicated dynamics of ego and depth psychology to the behaviour of groups continued to be illuminating. The idea of projection as an unconscious group activity is now widely used although not always remembered as one of Freud's original insights. Rationalization, part of the individual ego's process of secondary elaboration, occurs as another group mechanism clarified by Freud but rarely credited to him. In Britain current and overdue concern with racial prejudice provides examples of both these primitive defence mechanisms at a correspondingly primitive level. Freud recognized, in the undisguised antipathy and aversion which people so often feel towards strangers, and particularly identifiable strangers, who enter their community, a fundamental expression of the infantile, exclusive, self-love of narcissism. But he continued:

The element of truth behind all this, which people are so ready to disavow, is that men are not gentle creatures who want to be loved, and who at the most can defend themselves if they are attacked; they are, on the contrary, creatures among whose instinctual endowments is to be reckoned a powerful share of aggressiveness. As a result, their neighbour is for them not only a potential helper or sexual object, but also someone who tempts them to satisfy their aggressiveness on him, to exploit his capacity for work without compensation, to use him sexually without his consent, to seize his possessions, to humiliate him, to cause him pain, to torture and to kill him. . . .[63]

And how do people justify this when it happens? How do they justify to themselves the John Birch Society of America, the Ku Klux Klan, our own outrages at Notting Hill, the propaganda which underlay some of the political campaigning in the 1964 General Election at Smethwick? They justify them by the two convenient mechanisms of rationalization and projection. They rationalize their antipathy, not by acknowledging it to be basically entirely selfish, but by ascribing it to their love of justice or their sense of reality. 'It's not just that they're black (or Jewish – or Irish – or Dagos – or foreigners – or whatever they are), it's that there's no room for them here. We were here first, why should we let them into our schools, our hospitals. . . . We're not prejudiced; but they'd be much better off wherever it is they came from.'

The right of individuals to decide where they are to live and with whom they are to attempt to cooperate is clearly denied by this rationalization. It is then reinforced by projection. Anything which goes wrong in an area where unwelcome strangers have arrived is immediately blamed on them. The projections are often transparently absurd, but their absurdity is no barrier to the emotional satisfaction and justification which they appear to give. Local crime, particularly violence, unemployment, poor housing conditions, shortages, these are all 'their' doing. One sees the same thing even today when an attempt is made to build a new prison, a mental hospital or even a training and rehabilitation centre for mentally backward children. 'Why did they have to put that place here? It is only since they came that we've had all this trouble.' Even during the last few years, stillbirths in a local maternity hospital in England were blamed upon a special centre for mentally backward children which had recently been opened nearby. 'It was seeing those abnormal ones while they were pregnant that did it. . . .'

Beyond the Pleasure Principle: The Life and Death Instincts

Freud had been troubled by the inability of his original instinctual theory to account for certain aspects of human behaviour which seemed to go beyond the pleasure principle, in which the essentially conscious motivation of the ego, derived from the unconscious instinctual drives, was to seek pleasure in satisfaction of those drives. His definitive paper on this subject, intimations of which had appeared from time to time in earlier writings, was itself called *Beyond the Pleasure Principle* and was published in 1920. It has since been regarded as one of the most provocative and controversial of all Freud's works.

He began by reconsidering the economics or management of pleasure, following Fechner's biological principle of stability or constancy as the goal of a living organism, forerunner of Cannon's concept of homeostasis and Selye's adaptation theory, both of which postulate physiological equilibrium as the main task of physical life. Freud's own observations were remarkably far-sighted in this respect and, as always, arose from clinical observations on patients.

He instanced occasions on which the simple production of a state of pleasure by release of tension did not seem to fit the facts. Some he could explain by the existing hypothesis, but others seemed to demand a new theory. One of the first had been his observation that, in the course of normal fulfilment of sexual drive in final heterosexual union and orgasm, there was a constant tendency to delay and defer the achievement of orgasm, for just about as long as possible. He had noticed the same thing in the infant's determination in delaying and deferring the physical pleasure of emptying the bowel, not simply to demonstrate independence, but sometimes apparently for its own sake. Since the ultimate relief of tension was presumably the goal, why should human beings defer that goal when it was within reach? Freud came to the conclusion that this was simply to heighten and prolong the actual pleasure on the way to climax.

The attempt to make the act of union or the ultimate crescendo of pleasure last as long as possible led to what he called foreplay. This was a normal component of eroticism spreading out the active pleasure of release and fulfilment of libidinal drive. But there were other instances which could not be explained so easily.

Traumatic neuroses, following the severe environmental stresses of war or natural disaster, and previously completely misunderstood in the absence of any comprehension of the unconscious dynamic factors contributing to them, were never-theless still not fully explained by the existent theory of psycho-analysis. It was a great step forward to be able to substitute the concept of traumatic neuroses for meaningless terms like 'shell-shock', which had covered the total range of collapse under overwhelming stress in World War I. But what was much less satisfactory from Freud's standpoint was that in traumatic neuroses the traumatic events themselves continu-ally recurred in dreams which were productive of nothing but anxiety. The dream seemed to be failing in its primary func-tion. Often it did not even safeguard sleep. Never did it seem to achieve any resolution or release of conflict.

Patients would have repetitive dreams of terrifying situa-tions, often without any evidence of distortion at all, in which they would again be subjected to bombardment or buried alive, so that they came naturally to regard their dreams as among the most devastating of their symptoms. Eventually they might be unable to sleep for fear of what sleep and dreams would bring.

Freud also observed that in children there was an apparent compulsion whereby situations which the child could not tolerate were symbolized and constantly re-enacted. Freud's own grandson, Ernst, himself constructed a game in which he repeatedly re-enacted his own abandonment by his mother when she left him to go out. Freud recalled analyses of patients who appeared compelled to relive the anxiety-provoking situations of their childhood, without insight, transference or resolution occurring.

From these observations Freud abstracted the common hypothetical principle which he called 'repetition compulsion'. This repetition compulsion could sometimes be a simple application of the pleasure principle as, for example, when children wish to have the same story, which they already know by heart, read to them over and over again. But where the repetition was obviously far from pleasurable Freud saw in it the working through of an instinct for self-destruction. This led him to his concept of 'Thanatos', the 'death instinct'.

He defined the death instinct as a drive commonly encountered in nature to reinstate the former state of affairs. But in this case the ultimate aim of the drive is the return of organic or living matter to its inorganic unorganized state: life is but a preparation for death and has its own instinctual drive towards its end. The activity of the death instinct can only be deduced indirectly in most people. It is seen at its most obvious in the urge to self-destruction seen in compulsive and repeated suicidal attempts, in destructive habits such as unnecessary risk-taking, in alcoholism or drug addiction, or in the psychopathic pattern of the lives of those individuals who bring destruction upon themselves and everyone closely associated with them. Mildred, heroine of Somerset Maugham's novel *Of Human Bondage*, is a classic example, just as Phillip's hopeless and humiliatingly abject passion for her exemplifies his own compulsive projection and introjection. Indeed the concept of the death instinct has proved of far more use to artists and novelists than to clinicians, and was rejected by the vast majority of Freud's own disciples, seeming to them to be a senseless and contradictory idea. Freud himself was for a long time very hesitant about it:

It may be asked whether and how far I am myself convinced of the truth of the hypotheses that have been set out in these pages. My answer would be that I am not convinced myself, and that I do not seek to persuade other people to believe in them. Or precisely, that I do not know how far I believe in them.[64]

But although he was hesitant about it at first, he later became convinced of its value as a working hypothesis, and therefore of its clinical truth. He changed the concept of masochism, from being simply the reverse of the sadistic and dominant aspects of sadism in primitive sexuality, into being itself a primary instinct: a drive to embrace subjection and, finally, total subjugation and death. Aggression and submission were again heightened in importance in his total psychology. They were to receive final emphasis in his last and most speculative writings.

Finally, there were deeper reasons, partly personal, partly scientific, for the importance of this theory to Freud. From the foundation of psychoanalysis he had been trying to relate his brilliant hypotheses to physiological and biological processes. As early as the period immediately following the break with Breuer, Freud had hoped to be able to do this and had begun a series of essays called *A project for a Scientific Psychology* in 1895. But this was abandoned and never completed. Nevertheless it continued to haunt him, and in the death instinct he may well have considered that there was a natural correspondence between the inevitability of physical death and the drive of the human personality to accept this, even to seek it unconsciously, in a mixture of biological fulfilment and resignation.

The deficiencies in our description would probably vanish if we were already in a position to replace the psychological terms by physiological or chemical ones. It is true that they, too, are only part of a figurative language, but it is one with which we have long been familiar and which is perhaps a simpler one as well. . . .

Perhaps we have adopted the belief (the death instinct) because there is some comfort in it. If we are to die ourselves, and first to lose in death those who are dear to us, it is easier to submit to a remorseless law of nature, to the sublime necessity, than to a chance which might perhaps have been escaped. . . .[65]

With the concept of the death instinct, the libido had to be enlarged and magnified to balance it. It was then called the Eros or life instinct, and included all drives to survival as well as the instinctual sexual drive itself. But, whereas Freud had explored the ramifications of libido exhaustively, he was compelled to leave the death instinct as a concept which he himself could take virtually no further. Its development, its source, its impetus, its aim and its objects are all left relatively undiscussed. Aggression was clearly part of it, but the importance of aggression had now to be shifted to it, from its earlier association with sexual activity. The overtones of despair which characterize some of Freud's last writings about the future of the human race and its beliefs, while never losing either compassion or faith in the value of the individual, owe something to this daemonic concept which he himself had created or released, and which could bring so little comfort to him or to anyone else.

Some Further Views on Femininity

The importance to Freud himself of his final restatements on the topic of female sexuality probably derived as much from his earlier conviction, that women were almost a closed book to psychological inquiry,* as from any conspicuous contribution these views made either to the technique or the results of psychoanalysis itself. The views emerge in various papers but gain their most complete and technical expression in a paper entitled *Female Sexuality* published in 1931, and in the Lecture numbered 33 and entitled *Femininity* in *The New Introductory Lectures on Psychoanalysis* in 1933.

They consist in Freud's revision of his views about the Oedipus complex in so far as it affected women by postulating that, although infant boys and girls both shared the same incestuous phantasies about possession of their mothers, the latency period in girls was ushered in by a discovery that,

* Throughout his earlier writings Freud had made a number of general statements about the obscurity of feminine psychology. In the *Three Essays on Sexuality* in 1905 he wrote:

'The significance of the factor of sexual over-valuation can be best studied in men, for their erotic life alone has become accessible to research. That of women . . . is still veiled in an impenetrable obscurity.'[66]

In a paper published in 1923 on the phallic phase of sexual development he had stated:

'Unfortunately we can describe this state of things only as it affects the male child; the corresponding processes in the little girl are not known to us.'[67]

Three years later, in the long essay entitled *The Question of Lay Analysis*, we find these words:

'We know less about the sexual life of little girls than of boys. But we need not feel ashamed of this distinction; after all the sexual life of adult women is "a dark continent" for psychology . . .'[68]

And finally, in his opening to the essay which contains these further views on femininity, he has returned to the theme of what he calls 'the riddle' of the nature of femininity. Addressing his audience he says:

'Nor will *you* have escaped worrying over this problem – those of you who are men; to those of you who are women this will not apply – you are yourself the problem.'[69]

since neither they nor their mothers possessed a penis, they could never hope to gain fulfilment through identification with their mothers, that the wish for a penis was as doomed in their mothers' case as in their own. Their attachment to their fathers was therefore free of any innate threat, but their relationship with their mothers had to be abandoned together with projections of hostility towards them, repressed as phantasies that their mothers might wish to harm them.

Freud saw in the fondness for dolls of very young girls, under the age of five, simply a symbolic ownership of another creature over whom they could exert their power. The doll is both a symbol for a baby and a penis. By owning a doll the child makes herself a mother, but the mother is believed to be the owner of a penis herself, and so later, when this whole phantasy collapses in the face of reality, the girl transfers her hopes and her wishes to the father and rejects her mother, at least unconsciously. The antagonism which arises between girls and their mothers, particularly in adolescence, is probably a resurgence of this mechanism, still incompletely understood.

Freud believed that the achievement of mature femininity was more difficult for girls than was that of mature masculinity for boys. He postulated three possible lines of development from the end of the Oedipal stage of female infantile sexuality, only one of which would lead to normal femininity. The first two, both of which would result in abnormal development, were, respectively, total renunciation of sexuality with a more or less permanent fixation at a level of regressive infantile neurosis, and rejection of femininity in favour of a pseudo-masculine development.

In the first instance the child concludes that, since her clitoris is not a penis and never will be one, there is nothing she can hope for and nothing she can expect from sexuality. One modification of this will be her identification with her father as the only possible love object. Girls who never grow out of a wish to own their father have hysterical personalities, and thereby can suffer and inflict enormous suffering in their sexual and marital lives.

The second possibility involves a disorder of character in the direction of compensatory masculinity: the loss of the penis is denied and the whole of conscious life is led as though the girl were, in fact, still a boy and later a man. Tomboyism is the normal stage through which girls pass before leaving this behind; active lesbianism; or the hearty tweedy type of woman who wears no makeup, stands no nonsense and is generally unhappy and lonely, are the final outcome if fixation occurs at this stage.

The third possibility requires the girl to succeed in transferring her interest in a penis and her desire for a baby to the father, with phantasies of giving him a baby, so that ultimately she accepts female sexuality and the idea of union with a male only after leaving the father behind in the final emancipation of adolescence.

Freud offered some observations on the lessons of this analytic hypothesis in the actual understanding of feminine characteristics. As already foreseen, the choice of an adult partner in marriage may be the image of the father, or it may be the narcissistic ideal of the man whom the girl herself wished to become. Even when emancipation has been secured, Freud pointed out that in the lives of many women an unsettled, unresolved hostility, left behind in relationship to the mother, may re-emerge in the course of the daughter's married life and come finally to be projected on to the husband.

The woman's husband, who to begin with inherited from her father, becomes after a time her mother's heir as well. So it may easily happen that the second half of a woman's life may be filled by the struggle against her husband, just as the shorter first half was filled by her rebellion against her mother. . . .[70]

Evidence of Freud's own incompletely resolved Oedipus

complex can be detected in the concluding passages from this remarkable lecture on femininity:

A woman's identification with her mother allows us to distinguish two strata: the pre-Oedipus one which rests on her affectionate attachment to her mother and takes her as a model and the later one from the Oedipus complex which seeks to get rid of her mother and take her place with her father. . . .

It is in this identification (with her father) too that she acquires her attractiveness to a man, whose Oedipus attachment to his mother it kindles into passion. How often it happens, however, that it is only his son who obtains what he himself aspired to. . . .[71]

The envy of the penis remained for Freud an inseparable condition of unconscious female sexuality. To this he ascribed what he regarded as woman's relatively undeveloped sense of justice, itself related to the predominance of envy in her mental life:

For the demand for justice is the modification of envy and lays down the condition subject to which one can put envy aside. . . .[72]

He completes the essay with these words:

That is all I had to say to you about femininity. It is certainly incomplete and fragmentary and does not always sound friendly. But do not forget that I have only been describing women in so far as their nature is determined by their sexual function. It is true that that influence extends very far; but we do not overlook the fact that an individual woman may be a human being in other respects as well. If you want to know more about femininity, enquire from your own experience of life, or turn to the poets, or wait until science can give you deeper and more coherent information.[73]

Sublimation and Super-ego

Sublimation was Freud's hope for the creative future of humanity. He saw it as an alternative to neurosis, indeed as the alternative which creative man had always found when the dammed-back libido sought other paths for expression. He was not so foolish or so simple as to suggest that the energy displaced from sexual fulfilment, which went into the creation of works of art, was their sole source; nor did he pretend to himself or to others that the inquiring mind of the scientist, the creative touch of the sculptor or painter, or the imagination of the poet or novelist could be wholly explained by this mechanism. Indeed, as a man who had always stressed over-determination in the origin of human ideas and behaviour, it would have been wholly illogical, as well as obviously incomplete, to have made such a claim. But Freud did believe that the highest excursions of the human spirit, in the worlds of creative art and science, gained their impetus at the human level from the reserves of libidinal energy converted to their use.

Freud was explicit in disclaiming an over-all explanation for artistic talent shown in the products of genius through psychoanalysis. He said:

Since artistic talent and capacity are intimately connected with sublimation we must admit that the nature of the artistic function is also inaccessible to us along psychoanalytic lines. [74]

Freud's views on the psychodynamics of art were set out in one passage, written as early as 1916–17 in his *Introductory Lectures on Psychoanalysis*. He said there:

For there is a path that leads back from phantasy to reality – the path, that is, of art. An artist is once more in rudiments an introvert, not far removed from neurosis. He is oppressed by excessively powerful instinctual needs. He desires to win honour, power, wealth, fame and love of women; but he lacks the means for achieving these satisfactions. Consequently, like any other unsatisfied man, he turns away from reality and transfers all his interest, and his libido too, to the wishful constructions of his life of phantasy, whence the path might lead to neurosis. There must be, no doubt, a convergence of all kinds of things if this is not to be the complete outcome of his development; it is well known, indeed, how often artists in particular suffer from a partial inhibition of their efficiency owing to neurosis. Their constitution probably includes a strong capacity for sublimation and a certain degree of laxity in the repressions which are decisive for a conflict. An artist, however, finds a path back to reality in the following manner. To be sure, he is not the only one who leads a life of phantasy. Access to the halfway region of phantasy is permitted by the universal assent of mankind, and everyone suffering from privation expects to derive alleviation and consolation from it. But for those who are not artists the yield of pleasure to be derived from the sources of phantasy is very limited. The ruthlessness of their repressions forces them to be content with such meagre day-dreams as are allowed to become conscious. A man who is a true artist has more at his disposal. In the first place, he understands how to work over his day-dreams in such a way as to make them lose what is too personal about them and repels strangers, and to make it possible for others to share in the enjoyment of them. He understands, too, how to tone them down so that they do not easily betray their origin from proscribed sources. Furthermore, he possesses the mysterious power of shaping some particular material until it has become a faithful image of his phantasy; and he knows, moreover, how to link a yield of pleasure to this representation of his unconscious phantasy that, for the time being at least, repressions are outweighed and lifted by it. If he is able to accomplish all this, he makes it possible for other people once more to derive consolation and alleviation from their own sources of pleasure in their unconscious which have become inaccessible to them; he earns their gratitude and admiration and he has thus achieved *through* his phantasy what originally he had achieved only *in* his phantasy – honour, power and the love of women.[75]

Ego and Conscience

Just as sublimation is an attempt to explain the psychoanalytic contribution to art through the diversion of repressed libido into creative channels, so the concept of the super-ego, itself indispensable to the total of ego psychology, was used by Freud to explain the concept of human conscience, in terms of the experience of an individual of the authoritative, judgement-forming and punitive aspects of his parents, and others in positions of power during his childhood.

Conscience, said Freud, is in fact the operation of the judgements we have accepted from our parents when we were too young to question them, ultimately introjected into our own ego structure and then set up in authority as our own super-ego. We identify ourselves with these judgements and, whether we rebel against them or submit to them, they represent to us the guiding light, the principle on which we conduct our lives.

Freud, whose father had always been extremely important to him, was prepared to credit the super-ego with the ultimately significant role in forming the character structure of each generation of human beings.

It is easy to show that the ego-ideal answers in every way to what is expected of the higher nature of man. In so far as it is a substitute for the longing for a father, it contains the germ from which all religions have evolved. The self-judgement which declares that the ego falls short of its ideal produces the sense of worthlessness with which the religious believer attests his longing. As a child grows up, the office of father is carried on by masters and by others in authority; the power of their injunctions and prohibitions remains vested in the ego-ideal and continues, in the form of conscience, to exercise the censorship of morals. The tension between the demands of conscience and the actual attainments of the ego is experienced as a sense of guilt. Social feelings rest on the foundation of identifications with others, on the basis of an ego-ideal in common with them.[76]

From these statements, it becomes clear that Freud's explanation of the human conscience in terms of his concept of the super-ego, as derived essentially from the child's reaction to early environment and particularly to parental attitude and example, makes no provision for any inherent or absolute appreciation of right and wrong, and is in this sense independent of fundamental religious or moral significance.

For Freud this conclusion carried considerable force. Indeed he went on to treat the idea of God and the fact of religious belief as no more than projections of the child's relationship to his father, made in response to the wider stresses and threats of human existence, against which no human father could be expected to protect his son.

We are now at the end of this chapter and, tantalizingly enough, on the verge of one of the most acute paradoxes of the whole of the evolution of the theory of psychoanalysis. Super-ego judgements can have no inherent or absolute moral value: it is indeed part of the object of psychoanalysis itself to mitigate their effect. Yet to equate the super-ego with conscience, as Freud undoubtedly appeared to do, although he himself did disclaim any absolute knowledge in this respect, is to carry over into conscious thinking just those primitive over-simplifications characteristic of unconscious mental processes. It is moreover this very primitive and irrational quality of super-ego judgements which render them so demonstrably inadequate as a complete basis for conscience as a whole.

It is arguable that the ultimate source of morality, as experienced subjectively in conscience, must be something beyond individual tradition and environment if it is to be meaningful; it cannot be merely the distilled or distorted relics of infantile experience and environment. For by this thesis parental moral influence itself can have no deeper roots than the parent's own conscience, derived in turn from his parents before him; and the problem of the origin of values is shelved rather than solved by attributing the whole of one generation's morality to the conduct of their parents. Perhaps we reflect what is in us as well as what has been done to us. But before we can consider this further we have to turn to Freud's logical and inevitable application of his own views to the wider problems of human existence.

In Chapter 3 the quotation from the third of *Five Lectures on Psychoanalysis*, delivered in America and published in 1900, contained the statement by Freud that, if he was asked how one could become a psychologist, he would reply:

'By studying one's own dreams.'[77]

It was not long to remain as simple as that. But Freud's own analysis was accomplished in precisely this way and, in so far as it was ever completed, he himself was the only person who completed it. All his most fundamental discoveries, which enabled him to interpret the clinical material he observed in others, came from this self-exploration. What had begun as a personal intellectual inquiry had become an acute internal struggle, lasting from 1895 to well into the 1900s, and in one sense continuing all his life. The effect of this struggle was not simply to enable him to produce his theory of *The Interpretation of Dreams*, his sexual theories and the general theory of neuroses, it was also to convince him that no one who had not undergone a similar experience could reasonably attempt psychoanalysis. In 1910 he stated:

Now that a considerable number of people are practising psychoanalysis and exchanging their observations with one another, we have noticed that no psychoanalyst goes further than his own complexes and internal resistances permit; and we consequently require that he shall begin his activity with a self-analysis and continually carry it deeper while he is making his observations on his patients. Anyone who fails to produce results in a self-analysis of this kind may at once give up any idea of being able to treat patients by analysis.[78]

As he was subsequently to point out over and over again, this obligation was often not fulfilled by those who set themselves up as practitioners of psychoanalysis, and it would inevitably remain as a barrier to the understanding of psychoanalysis by the majority of interested readers. If this book proves itself to be only one more of a long list of failures to convey the essence of what Freud really said to those who wish to discover it, it may not simply be the author's incompetence; at least to some extent, it may be the unanalysed resistance of the readers which is responsible. This, of course, is a chance which every author has to take. Freud himself was to say categorically, and his followers have subsequently repeatedly insisted, that no unanalysed person can be expected fully to comprehend, still less to experience, the truth of psychoanalysis. Nevertheless, despite the greatness of Freud's own achievement, his self-analysis may well have been one of the most incomplete parts of all his work. The effect of his personality on the historical development of his subject cannot be exaggerated; but, as we shall see at the end of the book, it has the defects of its qualities.

Freud himself was never convinced that self-analysis was possible. In November 1897 he wrote to Fliess:

My self-analysis is still interrupted. I have now seen why. I can only analyse myself with the objectively acquired knowledge (as if I were a stranger): self-analysis is really impossible, otherwise there would be no illness. . . .[79]

And in a very revealing little aside in a paper on the subtleties of a parapraxis published in 1936, he added these words:

In self-analyses the danger of incompleteness is particularly great. One is too easily satisfied with a part-explanation, behind which resistance can easily keep back something which perhaps may be more important.[80]

Nevertheless, for a long time Freud regarded his own method of self-analysis as sufficient training for others. It was only when it became manifestly unsatisfactory that he was compelled to acknowledge the necessity for an alternative. This has since been made into a rigid requirement for analytic training (see comment Chapter 12, p. 194). The principal reasons for this were what Freud called counter-transferences: unforeseen and unanalysed feelings on the part of the analyst for the patient. Eventually, the conviction grew within the psychoanalytic movement that the only way to overcome these counter-transferences was by a personal analysis by a more experienced analyst. Personal analysis then became the absolute requirement of every analytic training institute. Commenting on this, a recent author of a book on Freud and his theories remarks aptly:

Where at first it was held that anybody could do what Freud had done, it was finally concluded that nobody could.* [81]

Whether Freud was actually able to do it himself remains inevitably a very open question. (See page 194.)

The final, and from Freud's point of view, entirely logical step, was characteristically proposed by Freud himself in *The Question of Lay Analysis*. This was his own major contribution to the problem of the organization of psychoanalysis between the wars. He believed that people could be trained and should be trained to practise psychoanalysis as a distinct discipline, quite independent of medical qualification.

It is, of course, absolutely characteristic of human beings when organized into any community that they should behave inconsistently as well as consistently. The medical profession were and are no exception. After doing everything they could to ridicule and deride Freud's theories in the early days, the profession later adopted them, without always acknowledging the need for the kind of training which Freud believed indispensable. Freud retaliated by writing his treatise on the ques-

* *Freud – A Critical Re-evaluation of his Theories* by Reuben Fine, 1962, p. 37.

tion of lay analysis, in which he attempted a fair discussion of
the case for and against lay analysis. The book takes the form
of a Socratic dialogue, in which Freud is the exponent, and an
impartial person, whom Freud had in mind but whose identity
he did not at the time disclose, is the critical recipient. The
book is still the classic argument in favour of permitting non-
medical people to practise analysis. Its shortcomings from the
standpoint of the author of this book will be reviewed in the
conclusion of this chapter.

Freud took up two positions which he steadfastly and
resolutely maintained. The first was that psychoanalysis was
primarily a branch of psychology and not of medicine. Privately he still regretted this, in so far as the project for a
scientific psychology had never proved possible for him. He
would have preferred the knowledge of chemistry, of biochemistry, physiology, anatomy and neurology in which he
had been trained, and to which he had himself contributed in
his earliest research, to have been indispensable to his subject.
But they were not: nor, at that time, could they even be related
to it. He therefore accepted the implications of the situation
and indeed had stated them implicitly at the foundation of the
International Psychoanalytical Association in 1910. The
principal object of this foundation was to make clear that
only certain people, who had accepted a full training, could be
accepted as qualified analysts and only on their work could the
work of psychoanalysis be judged.

His second point arises as a logical consequence of this:
namely that the proper practice of analysis can be acquired
only by a particular training, which in itself was not inherent
in the existing disciplines either of medicine or of psychology,
as they then were. Freud's own statement on this was succinct
and rigid:

I lay stress on the demand that no one should practise analysis
who has not acquired the right to do so by a particular training.

Whether such a person is a doctor or not seems to me immaterial.[82]

By this time Freud had an understandable bitterness towards many of his medical colleagues, not so much against them personally as against the attitude enshrined in their concept of medicine. They, not he, were the teachers of undergraduates; and he had a serious indictment with which to confront them. This was that medical education not only failed to instruct the future physician in psychology or in the techniques of psychoanalysis, but gave him a false and negative attitude towards the whole subject.

Everyone who has practised psychiatry from that day to this knows that what he said was true. Not everyone would agree with his conclusions, but no one would dispute the fairness and justice of their foundation. Freud's own conclusion was that, since the profession had failed to take up the challenge or study the issues, the challenge and the issues must be thrown open to anyone who cared enough to tackle and to study them. He maintained that this was necessary in the light of an objective consideration of three distinct interests: those of the patients, those of the medical profession and those of science.

As far as the patients were concerned, the history of their rejection by medicine and the total misunderstanding of the predicament of the hysteric, the patient with the anxiety state and the obsessional gave him all the evidence he needed. Sexual perverts and homosexuals completed the argument. These people needed understanding, not disapproval under the cloak of medical dogma.

From the standpoint of the medical profession, Freud simply said that if the qualified doctor wanted to be trained in psychoanalysis he would be a most acceptable candidate. If he did not, he could not thereby exclude others from that training or that opportunity. Since most doctors regarded the existent training as long enough already and few teachers would make room in medicine for analysis, Freud doubted whether the contribution of medicine would ever be sufficient for the demand of patients. The compulsory inclusion of psychoanalysis in the training of every doctor he considered both scientifically and economically impractical.

From the point of view of science, there remained his own hard-won conclusions about the grounds of psychoanalysis. These could be understood only by personal analysis. He believed personal analysis to equip the individual who undertook it, not simply for the treatment of neurosis, but for the understanding of the wider aspects of human life to be considered in the next chapter. But even from the standpoint of therapy itself, he felt that civilization's needs could never be met unless enough willing and carefully selected and trained recruits could be obtained from the population as a whole.

Our civilization imposes an almost intolerable pressure on us, and calls for a corrective. Is it too fantastic to expect that psychoanalysis, in spite of its difficulties, may be destined for the task of preparing mankind for such correctives? [83]

The main objection which modern psychiatry would raise to this thesis is simply that the differential diagnosis of many of the symptoms complained of by the patients whom Freud regarded as suitable for analysis, will require expert general assessment before they can safely be handed over to any exclusive specialist, whether medically qualified or not. Even in the most liberal approach, the exclusion or recognition of a brain tumour, progressive structural paralysis, impending haemorrhage from a peptic ulcer, the ravages of ulcerative colitis or of rheumatoid arthritis, are part of the clinical task of assessing symptoms often encountered in the neuroses, and cannot safely be undertaken by any but an experienced physician. Freud granted this, but implied that a physician should enter and leave the case at the discretion of the analyst.

Psychiatrists may accept the implications of this point of view, as doctors, without committing themselves to the support of lay analysis.

There remains one further consideration, already mentioned: the question of whether, even in suitable cases, analysis can always be regarded as a consistently conclusive procedure. Freud dealt with this in his paper on analysis terminable and interminable.

The purpose of this paper was to answer the question 'When can analysis be said to have been completed?' The simplest answer is, of course, when the symptoms disappear. However, Freud had already encountered what he called 'the flight into health'. This was not a cure, but rather an hysterical dissimulation, to bring an embarrassing aspect of treatment to a premature conclusion. Even if the symptoms have disappeared, there may still be character traits or conflicts which the patient and the analyst would wish to change, if the procedure were to continue. The ultimate goal of analysis, as Freud saw it, was to secure the best possible psychological equilibrium for the functioning of the ego, threatened and challenged on three sides as we have seen it to be: by the external environment, by the super-ego, and by the remorseless instinctual drives of the id.

The essential factors which Freud considered would determine whether analysis could in fact be successfully completed were three:

(1) The relative importance of the traumatic or triggering factor.

(2) The relative strength of the instinctual drives.

(3) The modifications of the ego in its attempt at defence.

When the traumatic factor is the decisive one, some degree of conclusive success can be hoped for in most cases. Even so, the traumatic neuroses provided an exception to this rule. But, for the most part, neuroses arising from the reactivation of stresses which would otherwise have been successfully contained can be analysed to completion within a relatively short time. In practice this may still mean months or even a year or more.

When the instinctual drives are both destructive to the equilibrium and to the ego and, at the same time, relatively stronger than its defences, then only an analysis which restores the theoretically possible equilibrium can succeed. Interviews for fifty minutes in the hour, one hour per day, five days a week, can go on for two or three years before this is achieved; and it may never be achieved except in those transference neuroses which have been carefully selected from the beginning.

But the final difficulty lies in the resources of the ego itself, and these involve biological considerations as well as psychological factors. Constitution, the hereditary background and other factors contributing to the total resilience of the human being concerned may be decisive. The tendency of the ego to take up wholly defensive or wholly dependent positions may make analysis impossible. Thrown back upon its own resources, the ego of a particular human being may find no answer in this attempt at self-sufficiency. To this analysis has no solution. Finally, and inevitably in Freud's own view, the death instinct of some individuals may ultimately be destined to triumph over all the instinctual drives serving Eros, the life instinct. Some people are doomed to self-destruction, and will use the efforts of others only either to delay or to complicate the end which they seek.

The emphasis here is on judgement, selection and flexibility in the analyst's conduct of his work. But he in turn acquires his training and qualifications in his own analysis. For practical purposes this must be relatively short and must be accepted as rarely being complete. Some analysts use their analysis as a defence and remain unchanged. Freud would have liked to have seen every analyst periodically undergo further analysis at intervals of five to ten years.

This would mean, then, that not only the therapeutic analysis of patients but his own analysis would change from a terminable into an interminable task. . . .[84]

Freud did not believe that all analysis was an endless procedure. What he has never said, but what has been said about analysis by those who support it objectively from without as well as from within the charmed circle of the institutes, is that *in practice it is suitable for perhaps one-tenth to one-twentieth* of all the people who consult their doctors in states of anguish and emotional distress. One of Freud's pupils already quoted, Ferenczi, commented that there were two conditions which must be resolved before analysis could be said to have been successful: they were penis envy in women, and total passivity in men. Freud felt this was asking too much; these conditions, he said, are biological facts, and the individual may still be enabled to live with them.

Many of Freud's followers consider *Analysis, Terminable and Interminable* to have been a pessimistic essay. Indeed there are many practising analysts who have succeeded in repressing the fact that they have ever read it. But in fact the wheel has come full circle. Freud's insight has illuminated, as it was bound to do, the fallibility of the human solution, as clearly as it illuminated the fallibility of the previous approaches to the human conflict and the nature of that conflict itself. Psychoanalysis had finally acknowledged its own fallibility.

Throughout his working life, Freud was not infrequently
astonished by his own deductions and conclusions; but,
while at first he may have been startled by them, he never
ultimately shrank from them, nor did he fail to pursue them
as far as he could to their logical conclusions. He had started
by wishing to be a man who would mould ideas, a worthy
leader of human society. In the purely theoretical sense, he
succeeded beyond his wildest expectations. This chapter will
concern itself with the opinions he expressed about the past
and future of mankind which, however controversial, followed
from his individual attention to the human predicament.

The works on which this chapter will be based are, respectively, *Totem and Taboo*, *The Future of an Illusion*, and
Civilization and its Discontents. At the end of his life Freud
wrote one more work relevant to this train of thought, namely
Moses and Monotheism. All these will contribute to our review.

At the beginning, Freud asked himself what contribution
his own knowledge could make to an understanding of man.
His immediate answer was that it provided a basis for psychological understanding of the individuals in any society. This
does not mean that psychoanalysis is the final answer to everything in human life. In *Totem and Taboo* Freud specifically
disclaimed this, insisting that the psychoanalytic aspect must
be considered as one of many.

There are no grounds for fearing that psychoanalysis, which first
discovered that psychical acts and structures are invariably over-
determined, will be tempted to trace the origin of anything so
complicated as religion to a single source. If psychoanalysis is
compelled – and is, indeed, in duty bound – to lay all the

emphasis upon one particular source, that does not mean it is claiming either that the source is the only one or that it occupies first place among the numerous contributory factors. Only when we can synthesize the findings in the different fields of research will it become possible to arrive at the relative importance of the part played in the genesis of religion by the mechanism discussed in these pages. Such a task lies beyond the means as well as beyond the purposes of a psychoanalyst.[85]

The sub-title of *Totem and Taboo* was *Some points of agreement between the mental life of savages and neurotics*. This exemplifies the thesis.

The book is in fact a collection of four essays. The first, called *The Horror of Incest*, reviews the anthropological literature on the subject of incest with which Freud had made himself familiar. He pointed out that it was a stronger taboo among primitive people than in more civilized communities and that it could be so extensive as to lead to a system of exogamy, whereby both men and women in a tribe were compelled to seek their sexual partners outside the tribe altogether. Exogamy he considered to be closely related to totemism; wherever totems are to be found, there is also a law against persons belonging to that totem having sexual relations with each other, and consequently against their marrying.

What is a totem? It is an animal, usually one familiar to the tribe, but forbidden to be hunted because it is regarded as containing the essence of the tribal god. On one occasion only during the year may this animal be killed, in what is in fact a sacramental rite. Following this ritual sacrifice of the totem animal, it is eaten by the tribe, and in fact the entire ritual is an avowal of their taking into themselves the qualities which it symbolizes. At no other time of the year may the animal be either hunted, slain or, above all, eaten. The ambivalence of this procedure, whereby something which is forbidden at all other times is compulsive on a particular occasion, is not only part of the mystery but also part of the power underlying the totem itself. Totem poles in primitive tribes are simply effigies carved in the likeness of the animal and its attributes, which are set up as reminders of the meaning and sacred nature of the totem object.

In the second essay of the collection, entitled *Taboo and Emotional Ambivalence*, Freud draws attention to the remarkable similarity between the religious practices of totemism and the obsessional acts and beliefs of neurotic patients. He points out that these were so marked that if the term 'obsessional neurosis' had never been invented in Western civilization it could have been translated entirely from primitive tribes by calling it 'taboo sickness'. It is in fact a system of ritual expiation directed against guilt incurred in the mind of the individual, by the conviction that the rule of the totem has been broken. This rule, Freud reminded his readers, was a sexual rule, the rule against incest. Obsessional neuroses are a defence against incestuous wishes and rebellions of childhood; religious practices are a defence against the same fear, now spread among the entire community as a sense of guilt for their aggressive and rebellious wishes against the sexual morality of their community.

His illustrations here are telling. Ambivalence, already seen to be part of totemism, is of course deeply inherent in an obsessional neurosis. The forbidden act sometimes has to be performed: one is reminded of the Rat Man, who feared that, if he either paid or did not pay the money for the delivery of his spectacles to a particular person, his father and the woman he loved would suffer the rat torture. Finally, he had to make an actual decision as to which was the propitious thing to do. He chose to pay the money, but in the end in fact never paid it. Here obsessional doubt prevented the completion of the ritual.

Projection, another element of neurotic thought and behaviour already familiar to psychoanalysis, was equally clear in totemism. The attributes of a god, that is, the super-ego, in this case the collective super-ego of the tribe, are projected on to the animal. This preserves the animal for 364 days of the year and condemns it for the 365th. Ambivalence and projection could hardly be better exemplified. Totem tribes also institute scapegoats, that is, other animals or occasionally prisoners of tribal warfare, on whom are projected all the guilt and apprehension of the tribe, which are finally removed by driving the animal or the prisoner out of the village or by hunting and killing it, thereby expiating the communal sense of impending retribution.

While emphasizing these similarities, Freud also remarked the essential difference between totem and taboo on the one hand and neuroses on the other. Neurosis, he said, is both socially disapproved and related to private sexual anguish. Taboo is socially approved and is related to public social prohibition.

The third essay bears the title *Animism, Magic and the Omnipotence of Thoughts*. In this Freud took up an account which was accepted in his day as the explanation of the evolution of human views of the universe. An animistic phase came first, a religious phase second and a scientific phase third and finally. He explained these phases in terms of the omnipotence of thoughts, already encountered in his analyses of obsessional patients, and particularly the Rat Man. This omnipotence is seen in the phantasies of childhood: if you think something, it is more likely to happen than if you don't. Not thinking of things makes them less likely.

This is known to be part of the philosophy of primitive tribes. The most primitive regard thoughts as equivalent to deeds or facts. Later, they transfer this appalling power from themselves to their gods, but this enables them to retain the idea of omnipotence, by intercession. Finally, omnipotence has to give way to the objective scientific study of probability. Men deal with reality and abandon their belief in magic, and the power of their thoughts, to influence the real world. Omnipotence survives only in fairy tales, in childhood, in neurosis and in dreams. For Freud, therefore, religion was the survival of a tribal neurosis.

The final essay of the series was called *The Return of Totemism in Childhood*. This contained the theory which provoked the major anthropological criticism of Freud's attempt to contribute to this source of knowledge, although it was based in fact on what were perfectly respectable sources at the time whcn Freud relied upon them.

No less a master than Darwin had proposed the hypothesis that primitive man, like the higher apes, had lived in hordes in which one male was the father of the tribe, with many wives and a very largc number of children. The young males were forced out of the tribe to find mates, and the young females could expect no mate but the leader of the horde. This would obviously be a disagreeable situation, to both the young women and the young men of the tribe. Freud suggested that the young men had in fact risen in a body to murder their father and gain possession of his women. But once they had done this they were overcome by a tremendous collective sense of guilt and a need for expiation. From this arose their endowment of the totem with the qualities of the previous father-leader of the tribal horde, the preservation of this animal throughout the year, and yet the commemoration of the act of liberation by its ritual sacrifice and consumption on the special day of each tribal feast.

The function of the totem here would be to remind the tribe as a whole that the single authority of the father had gone, at a human level, but that it must be preserved at a religious level. Similarly, in order to avoid repeated internecine tribal warfare and competition for the available women, incest, that is marrying within the families within the tribe, would have to be prohibited and a relative degree of exogamy reconstituted. No longer would the men be expelled fom the tribe and the women remain the property of one man; instead the men would have to work together, bound by their mutual sense both of guilt and of responsibility, while the women of the family would have to accept marriage only to men of other families than their own. The prohibition against internecine strife and incest would thus be safeguarded by totem and taboo; but by this time these would have become repressed in the individual consciousness of members of the tribe and enforced upon them by their priests who, as keepers of their mysteries, would in fact be reminding them of a collective guilt and a universal super-ego judgement introjected into all of them, stemming from the original act of murder. This was how Freud conceived the final common basis of religion.

Summing up this situation, Freud says once again that the Oedipus complex is in fact universal. Everywhere men must be prevented from desiring their mothers and wishing to kill their fathers.

At the conclusion, then, of this exceedingly condensed inquiry, I should like to insist that its outcome shows that the beginnings of religion, morals, society, and art converge in the Oedipus complex. This is in complete agreement with the psychoanalytic finding that the same complex constitutes the nucleus of all neuroses, insofar as our present knowledge goes. It seems to me a most surprising discovery that the problems of social psychology, too, should prove soluble on the basis of one single concrete point – man's relation to his father.[86]

Did Freud believe this to be a historical account? The answer to this is that he did and at the same time he didn't. He writes about the possibilities and probabilities, the unlikelihood and at the same time the certainty that this was part of the original mental inheritance of the human race. In a sense, he tends at this stage both to display ambivalence and to plead poetic licence. Whether it happened or not, it is important, because it corresponds to the myths and dreams of all the human race. If it corresponds to the myths and dreams of all the human race, it must have happened. Freud the mythmaker has come a long way from Freud the scientist.

Totem and Taboo was published in 1914, and therefore
missed most of the Western world, who were engaged in
fighting against Germany and Austria. But even when it
reached them, the reader will not be surprised to discover
that it was one of Freud's least popular works, although it is
probably one of his most original and creative essays.

By 1927, Freud was ready to proceed again with this thesis,
whose personal importance to him was particularly significant.
He wrote then a small monograph entitled *The Future of an
Illusion*, and followed it up three years later with a larger book,
Civilization, and its Discontents. We can relate these two books
to each other, and see what was their basic message.

In essence, Freud dismissed the idea of God as an illusion,
created by humanity to comfort them in the face of their helplessness when they have outgrown their parents. Original
sin and a sense of guilt, he said, were in fact related to the
primitive and inherited shame, going back to the original act
of murder described in *Totem and Taboo*, when the sons of the
tribe rebelled against the father-leader, killing him to gain
possession of the women. Freud was no longer disposed to
argue whether this was likely, or acceptable. Upon this thesis
he based the dual contention that religion was in fact an illusion, and ought to be abandoned, while at the same time concluding, frankly and reluctantly, that mankind was not yet
ready for the challenge implied by this liberation from superstition. Indeed, he commented sadly, the worship of God and
the belief in an absolute system of values belonging to Him
was perhaps a necessary fiction to preserve some semblance of
law and order until the human race had advanced sufficiently
in wisdom to do without any of the illusions to which it had
hitherto clung. In *Civilization and its Discontents* he re-
examines the need for these illusions in terms of man's instinctual drives and their outcome. Suffering, he says, is
unfortunately universal. We suffer either from our bodily predicament, because of pain from injury or disease, or we suffer

from dangers which we have to avoid in our external environment or, finally, we suffer because of our relations with our fellow-men. As has already been indicated on page 155 our fellow-men finally constitute the greatest danger.

For civilization to exist, said Freud, we have to surrender most of our instinctual drive for sexual and personal freedom. The claims of the individual and the claims of the community will always be in conflict. However, at this stage, Freud rather surprisingly does not regard sexual privations as the most acute. Most men and most women, he thought, could obtain a sexual partner and sexual satisfaction and gain thereby their own personal equilibrium, if sufficiently emotionally mature and stable, without too much interference from society. What they cannot bear are their neighbours.

The reason for this is that men are in fact aggressive, self-assertive and uncharitable. Freud examined sanctions of religion directed towards the control of this obviously explosive situation. For the Christian commandment, 'Thou shalt love thy neighbour as thyself', which he considered frankly impracticable, and which was followed by the even more stringent commandment, 'Love thine enemies', he suggested as an alternative that each individual might attempt to become more fully aware of his own repressed conflicts and the urge to aggression in himself, with the object of pursuing a policy of enlightened self-interest. This might enable him to live at peace with others, once he realized that his instinctual urge to dominate or attack them must have as its final deterrent only the possibility that, having the same urge, they would do the same to him, thus rendering society chaotic and vulnerable to every form of personal vendetta or tribal war. The race would go to the swift, booty to the strongest; murder, violence, rape and incest would re-emerge if taboos were overthrown but enlightenment did not suffice to take their place.

How could civilization be expected to hold this essentially unstable equilibrium in being? Only by a communal renunciation of instinctual gratification, which any community would have to make as the price of its continued existence. The renunciation of aggression is the hardest privation of all. Freud hoped that while culture might mitigate the severity of this renunciation, the inevitable suffering inseparable from the resolution of this process was no more than could already be observed in everyday life. Guilt, particularly communal guilt, would be one way of enforcing this renunciation. The easiest way to make it effective would be to displace the aggression from the ego to the super-ego, and then to introject the super-ego not simply into each individual but into the community, into their communal values and beliefs. In fact a new system of ethics would have to take the place of the old; and it is hard to see how psychoanalysis itself could escape the invidious distinction of becoming a new religion.

Meanwhile, said Freud, the individual super-ego will probably be inversely harsh in proportion to the conduct of its possessor. The more aggressive human beings become in their outward actions, the more permissive must be their super-ego; the more severe and punitive their super-ego, the more humble their outward behaviour must become.

Throughout the whole of this paper, Freud writes as though he were thinking aloud and had not reached firm conclusions in his own mind. His vision is a mournful one, and its principal redeeming feature is the mixture of compassion and patience which he is prepared to extend to society, and which one may gather was derived from the attitude which he had already learned to extend towards his patients. Indeed, while his final conclusion is that the price of culture and civilization is individual suffering and the renunciation of instinctual drives towards individual satisfaction, he holds out the tenuous hope that the neurosis of culture may itself derive from the punitive nature of a collective super-ego which may one day become accessible to communal analysis.

Freud's last contribution to this type of speculative theory was *Moses and Monotheism*. This is the last book he ever completed; it was re-written in various forms a number of times. The book as it now remains contains two separate openings, both written in Austria, on the eve of the Nazi take-over of that country. The last section, as drafted, was never intended for publication at all and was finally combined with the first two and published only after Freud had reached England and safety, on the eve of the outbreak of World War II. The second part of the book contains a touching reference to the kindness of his welcome in.

. . . lovely, free, magnanimous England. Here I now live, a welcome guest; I can breathe a sigh of relief now that the weight has been taken off me and that I am once more able to speak and write – I had almost said 'and think' – as I wish or as I must. I venture to bring the last portion of my work before the public. . . .[87]

The first part of the essay, twice re-written, was the thesis that Moses was not a Jew but an Egyptian and that the strict monotheism characteristic of Judaism was derived from the teachings of the Egyptian King Akhenaton, a heretic in the tradition of the Egyptian religion, in that he was most merciful and loving. Freud believed that the Jews in fact murdered Moses, following the pattern of the murder of the father-leader of the tribal horde, and that thereafter they oscillated between obedience to and hatred for the remembered image of this primordial figure. He went on to suggest that their motive for adopting the religion taken from this leader was precisely the same as that actuating the sons of the primal horde in *Totem and Taboo*. He concluded his essay with the part written in England, including some reflections on anti-semitism which have a poignant ring.

No other portion of the history of religion has become so clear to us as the introduction of monotheism into Judaism and its continuation in Christianity – if we leave on one side the development which we can trace no less uninterruptedly, from the animal totem to the human god with his regular companions. (Each of the four Christian evangelists still has his own favourite animal.) If we provisionally accept the world-empire of the Pharaohs as the determining cause of the emergence of the monotheist idea, we see that that idea, released from its native soil and transferred to another people was, after a long period of latency, taken hold of by them, preserved by them as a precious possession and, in turn, itself kept them alive by giving them pride in being a chosen people: it was the religion of their primal father to which were attached their hope of reward, of distinction and finally of world-dominion.[88]

Nevertheless, the Jews carried with them the guilt of the murder of Moses, and in Freud's opinion had become an indispensable part of the repressed historical recollection of mankind, an important link between the forgotten deed in primeval times and its subsequent reappearance in the form of monotheistic religions. Freud suggested that the guilt attached to the murder of Moses may indeed have been the stimulus for what he called the wish phantasy of the Messiah, who was in turn to give to his people salvation and the promised sovereignty over the world.

The poor Jewish people, who with its usual stiff-necked obduracy continued to deny the murder of their 'father', has dearly expiated this in the course of centuries. Over and over again they heard the reproach: you killed our God. And this reproach is true, if rightly interpreted. It says, in reference to the history of religion: 'you won't admit that you murdered God' (the archetype of God, the primeval Father and his reincarnations). Something should be added, namely: 'It is true, we did the same thing, but we admitted it, and since then we have been purified.'

Not all accusations with which anti-semitism pursues the descendants of the Jewish people are based on such good foundations. There must, of course, be more than one reason for a phenomenon of such intensity and lasting strength as the popular hatred of Jews. A whole series of reasons can be divined: some of them, which need no interpretation, arise from obvious considerations; others lie deeper and spring from secret sources, which one would regard as the specific motives. . . .[89]

Freud believed that these motives included the difference of Jews from their hosts, in that they are the remnants of a Mediterranean people with an inherited and closely preserved culture. Moreover they defy oppression, and even the most cruel persecutions have not succeeded in exterminating them. On the contrary, they have shown a capacity for holding their own in practical life and, wherever they are admitted, for making valuable contributions to the surrounding civilization.

The deeper origins of anti-semitism Freud traces to the unconscious acceptance by other people that they were in fact in some way a favoured people, children of God the Father, and were therefore blamed for what is consciously denied about them: sibling rivalry occurring here in racial relations. Also there is an indication of aloofness which can be traced through the history of their race. At one time they were regarded as a people singularly subject to leprosy, and were ostensibly dreaded because they might bring leprosy into the communities in which they lived. In fact Jews have never been specifically vulnerable to this illness, and in Freud's view it is more probable that this is a displacement and, indeed, a reversal of an unconscious kind. The Jews, by holding themselves aloof, imply that other people are lepers; and this is resented. The resentment is displaced and projected on to them together with its ostensible cause.

Finally, there are two things about them which make them inspire hostility and dread: the first is that they are circumcized, which reminds others of the dreaded castration idea, and of things in their primeval past they would prefer to forget. The second is that many Christian anti-semites are only thinly Christian: under this veneer is their older, more primitive religion, and they have not yet overcome their grudge against this new religion forced upon them, which they project on to the source from which Christianity reached them. The fact that the Gospels tell a story enacted among Jews and treating of Jews may have facilitated this projection. 'Their hatred of Jews,' concludes Freud, 'is at bottom a hatred of Christians, and we need not be surprised that in the German National-Socialist revolution this intimate relation between the two monotheist religions finds such a clear expression in the hostile treatment of both of them.'[90]

We have finished our examination of what Freud really said, in rather less than one fiftieth of the volume of his original published work. It is fitting to pay him the respect he would have been glad to acknowledge, by venturing some final and personal observations on his remarkable ideas.

The first indications of psychoanalysis were contained in the preliminary communication of *Studies in Hysteria*, published in 1893 when Freud was thirty-seven. From then until his death in 1939 he produced the three-and-a-half million words on which this book – and, indeed, many other books – has been based.

As well as the subjects indicated in the eleven preceding chapters, Freud wrote widely and on a large number of topics. Many of these were technical but some were highly personal and revealing. They included essays inspired by his travels and an *Autobiographical Study*. A Standard Edition of his complete works is included in the Appendix. His monograph on *Jokes and the Unconscious* has already been mentioned. In a similar vein were several essays on the application of psychoanalytical methods to the interpretation of art and artists such as Leonardo da Vinci and the Moses of Michelangelo, and he devoted one monograph, *Gradiva – Delusion and Dream*, to the analysis of the dreams of a character in the novel by Jensen whose title he included in his own. Despite the obvious inability of the character concerned to supply Freud with free associations to the manifest content of his dreams, the master records his delight, but not surprise, at the realization that the content, mechanisms and meaning of the dreams attributed to this character fitted perfectly with the psychopathology revealed by the character's actions and experiences throughout the novel as a whole. He maintained steadfastly that the artist was able, and in one sense was bound, to reflect with fidelity and precision those workings of the mind of which he might know nothing from a scientific standpoint, but which his heightened sensitivity enabled him to discover on an intuitive basis. In this way a true artist could create characters of a depth and complexity which were all the more striking and impressive because their analysis along strictly scientific lines proved them to have as consistent and valid a relationship with psychoanalytic theory as had the psychopathological structure of living people.

Now all this makes very stimulating reading and adds a whole chapter of possibilities to the scope of literary criticism, but on the purely scientific basis on which Freud took his stand the inherent fallacy is obvious. The analysis of the dreams of real people makes it clear that only the free associations of the patient, and not the projections and interpretations of the analyst, can lead to a full understanding of the case.

The fallacy of analysing the creation of an artist's imagination is that one's own imagination inevitably fills in the gaps which genius always leaves in a character for that very purpose. To attempt to analyse a human being we need all the help that human being can give us; and no analysis which rested purely upon a study of the dreams or the history of the person, without his association or comments upon them, could claim to be complete. None the less, as a technique for literary criticism which is often productive of an original and provocative treatment, and as a refreshing form of relaxation for psychiatrists themselves, there is a great deal to be said for this procedure, provided always that we do not take its results or ourselves unduly seriously. Was Freud making this mistake? In this context, I venture to think not. But it helps to remind us that he was human – and therefore not always consistent.

Bearing this in mind we can – and must – ask some questions and permit ourselves to speculate about their answers in much the same way that Freud himself, much to our edification and instruction, permitted himself to speculate about Moses, Leonardo da Vinci and the character in *Gradiva*.

The first question concerns the foundation and subsequent hierarchical structure of the psychoanalytic movement itself. It has been described, not unduly harshly, as having

. . . come to resemble a cult more than a scientific discipline. It has its canonical literature, its apocryphas, its orthodoxies and heterodoxies, its inquisitors and its apostolic succession. Orthodox psychoanalysts are compelled to submit their will and reason to as stern a discipline as any members of a religious order. Thus it comes about that many psychoanalysts inhabit a little world of their own that is apt to be quite out of touch with systems of thought which are foreign to them. For instance, they find it difficult to believe that there are still countless thousands of well-educated people who are completely unfamiliar with psychoanalytical theory and practice. If they were told that there were also a great number of people who were well acquainted with psychoanalysis and who found themselves quite unable to accept its dogmata, they would say that such people are either intellectually dishonest or require to be analysed in order to overcome their own psychic resistances.[91]

Yet the whole of this sincerely imposing edifice rests upon a paradox, if not an outright fundamental contradiction.

We have already glimpsed its nature (pages 171–5). The movement, founded by Freud himself, is dedicated to the proposition that no one can truly understand or practice psychoanalysis unless he or she has first been analysed; and that no one can analyse himself. But Freud never submitted himself to analysis by a colleague. Why not?

There can be only one answer consistent with his own theories. As the father of the horde, he could be sacrificed but not saved. Without an invitation from him, none of his followers presumed to offer to complete his analysis: nor in his turn did he choose to submit himself to their attentions.

So he remains the exception which defies the rule – and defies it for ever.

There is an amusing but almost certainly apocryphal tale about an attempt at mutual analysis between Freud and Jung which supposedly contributed to their ultimate disagreement and separation, but this is clearly irrelevant. So, allowing for Freud's own dictum that no analysis is ever finally complete, just how finally incomplete was his own self-analysis? And what is the relevance of this to his work as a whole?

This is not a flippant question; nor is it disrespectful to the genius of the man. It is in fact exactly the sort of question he would have asked himself. There can of course be no final answer: but there are important indications, and we can briefly consider them.

Until some time after his father's death, Freud considered himself subject to symptoms of neurosis. His feelings for his father and mother were as profound and complicated as his own theories would suggest; his father was an orthodox Jew and, throughout his father's life as well as his own, he had seen the vicious power of racial intolerance – in this case anti-semitism – to humiliate, insult and embitter social and professional relationships.

He was understandably critical of the idea of political authority, and entirely rejected the concept of spiritual authority: nor was he ever able to overcome a certain wariness and hesitancy on the subject of women (pages 160 *et seq.*). Occasionally there were curious lapses in his usually meticulous scholarship. The riddle of the Theban Sphinx provides an interesting example.

This formed part of the original Oedipus myth. The tragedy is set in Thebes, birthplace of Oedipus, who on his unrecognized return found the country terrorized by the Sphinx, who asked everyone encountering it a riddle, killing them when they could not answer. Oedipus answered the riddle and broke the creature's spell. What was the riddle – and what was the answer?

Freud says the riddle was, 'Where do babies come from?' (*An Autobiographical Study*, Standard Edition, p. 37)[92] and leaves the answer to our imagination. But the classical version of the riddle is quite different. It was:

'Which is the animal that has four feet in the morning, two at midday and three in the evening?' Oedipus answered: 'Man, who in infancy crawls on all fours, who walks upright on two feet in maturity, and in his old age supports himself with a stick.' The Sphinx was vanquished and threw herself into the sea.[93]

The actual answer would certainly not have lacked a Freudian interpretation: the stick and the third leg are obvious enough symbols. So why the confusion?

Again we can only speculate: the question about babies is a child's question to his mother; Freud leaves us in no doubt about its importance to him. In his own childhood may it have been unanswered? – or believed by him to be unanswerable? – or even one he dared not ask? The resemblance to the predicament of Little Hans (page 141) is certainly impressive. But even the recovery of Little Hans has received an alternative explanation from the behaviourist school (page 143). Freud deplored behaviourism. Its crude mechanistic beginnings in the dawn of the twentieth century had only one feature in common with the philosophical basis of psychoanalysis: a reliance on determinism as the final foundation of scientific method.

We cannot consider behaviourism further here, but we can trace an important observation of Freud himself on the deterministic basis of psychoanalysis. It is an example of his scientific honesty and objectivity at its best, inasmuch as it contains no speculation, no special pleading and no tendency to gloss over a failure, which he himself could have found no satisfaction in acknowledging. He is writing of a particular case:

But at this point we become aware of a state of things which also confronts us in many other instances in which light has been thrown by psychoanalysis on a mental process. So long as we trace the development from its final stage backwards, the connexion appears continuous, and we feel we have gained an insight which is completely satisfactory and even exhaustive. But if we proceed the reverse way, if we start from the premises inferred from the analysis and try to follow these up to the final result, then we no longer get the impression of an inevitable sequence of events which could not be otherwise determined. We notice at once that there might have been another result, and that we might have been just as well able to understand and explain the latter. The synthesis is thus not so satisfactory as the analysis; in other words, from a knowledge of the premises we could not have foretold the nature of the result.[94]

Nor did Freud press the claims of psychoanalysis as an exclusive therapeutic technique: he was content to leave to others the attempt to justify it by results in terms of figures of patients treated and improved.*

But he was concerned to dispel avoidable errors about psychoanalysis. Two which survived his efforts unchanged were those surrounding the ideas of sex and repression, and those which equated the analytic couch with the Catholic confessional. Of these the former is the more ignorantly vulgar:

* The published results of the Berlin Psychoanalytic Institute from 1920 to 1930 (referred to by Freud in *New Introductory Lectures on Psychoanalysis*, 1932–6, S. E. XXII, p. 152, and *The Preface to Ten Years of the Berlin Psycho-Analytic Institute* (1930), S.E. XXI, p. 257), are interesting in this respect. They are set out below:

Total of patients taken into treatment (1920–30)   312
Total of patients who completed treatment (1920–30)   200†
Percentage recovered or improved –
     of all taken on   58%
     of those who completed analysis   91%

† The difference between 312 and 200 represents the number of patients (112) who, after entering into psycho-analytic treatment, broke it off or gave it up for one reason or another.

whereby repression is assumed to mean discipline (parental discipline in childhood, self-discipline in adult life) instead of an unconscious process, and Freud is then accused of advocating unbridled sexual licence as a cure for neurosis. The absurdity of this needs no further exposition for anyone who has read this far.

The second error is scarcely less naïve, though certainly less popular because less salacious. To compare the couch to the confessional is to ignore the fact that the proclaimed purpose of confession is to deal with conscious guilt about voluntary and deliberate wrongdoing, by asking God's forgiveness for admitted sins; whereas the object of analysis is to bring into consciousness hitherto repressed and unconscious feelings, and to deal with involuntary phantasies more often than with frank intentions or actual deeds. The two are therefore fundamentally different. Much of what Freud really said was directed towards demonstrating the essential fallacy of regarding conscious and unconscious mental life as directly comparable.

Psychoanalysis, regarded as a method of study, a technique for treatment and research, or as the body of knowledge which this method and technique have uncovered, has certain solid claims which are beyond dispute. Moreover, as a method which has produced results, it can claim an empirical justification and a certain scientific respectability. The original clinical studies in hysteria, the remarkable interpretation of dreams, the whole concept of depth psychology, the sexual theories and the general theory of the neuroses, all these can stand examination on their merits. By contrast the philosophical theories, beginning with the concept of the death instinct and proceeding to the origins of morality and religion, emerge as simply the unfettered speculations of their originator, eminently worth reading for the sake of the light which they shed on the personality of Freud himself, but still no more than speculations.

Nevertheless, once he had propounded them, Freud displayed a remarkably uncharacteristic dogmatism in upholding them; an attitude which, had he encountered it in anyone else, would have suggested to him the strong possibility of an emotional rather than an objective scientific basis for the development of the ideas. We may wonder whether his own unresolved conflict and intensely charged feelings about his father, and his background of paternal race and creed, were not perhaps as much responsible for his views about conscience and religion, particularly as exemplified by the Jewish and Christian idea of the personal God, as were any of his scientific abilities.

Be that as it may, it remains true that Freud could claim no more authority for his conclusions in this respect than could be claimed for the subjective speculations of anybody else. His brilliant ability to explain how the idea of God and the idea of fatherhood might be linked in the human mind, and how both ideas could be expected to become involved in the developing conscience of the individual, is in no sense an answer to the wider and infinitely more important question of why the concept of God should be a part of human mental existence at all.

Nor can any hypothesis, no matter how valid or convincing, about the way in which beliefs occur, affect the essential validity of these beliefs themselves. To challenge the fundamental validity of religious belief it is necessary to examine closely its whole substance and meaning; yet this is precisely what Freud could never bring himself to do. This omission is significant; not least in the light of his own theories.

Roland Dalbiez, the French philosopher and profound student of psychoanalysis, has written in this context that Freud has nowhere proved or even sought to prove that religious belief is in fact illusory. His writings may be sought in vain for such proof. We find certain peremptory and unsupported assertions concerning the incompatability of science and religion, but Freud has no argument to adduce on the very foundation of the problem. 'Nor,' says Dalbiez,

. . . is it obvious how, whatever may be one's personal solution of the religious problem, one could show that religion is a delusion. For a delusion is not only a false belief – otherwise all error would be delusional – it is an irreducible belief which is obviously false. Once we cease to deal with immediate evidence and common sense certainty, the application of the concept of delusion becomes a matter of some difficulty. . . . If the atheistic psychiatrist wants to remain faithful to the requirements of a strict methodology, he must regard religious belief, not as a delusion in the psychiatric meaning of the word, but as a conviction which he holds to be false because of his own personal philosophy.[95]

In fact psychoanalysts are not all atheists; some are Jews, some are Christians. But all psychoanalysts recognize that even after complete and successful analysis the subject has still no more than his own individual human resources upon which to rely. And in fact, as we have already seen (page 177), these are not always enough. Sometimes the conflicts of which the subject becomes aware remain insoluble for him: this is the crisis in analysis; and within its own framework analysis has no answer. The patient, groping beyond himself for further help, cannot get it from the analyst; for no transference can be maintained for a lifetime. Yet at this point the patient whose quest for faith is limited to himself or to his analyst may be hopelessly stranded. This is but one aspect of the problem of the interminable analysis as foreseen by Freud himself.

But perhaps this in itself emerges as only one more special example of the ultimate predicament of man, for whom full self-awareness and self-realization are never by themselves entirely enough. Nevertheless it was Freud's contention that they had to be sufficient: because they were all that man had, or could ever have. Writing of this in his conclusion to his own exposition and critique of Freud's theories, Dalbiez ends with these words:

If we wish to have an idea of the greatness of Freud's work, we must turn primarily to the analysis of dreams. There have been dreams ever since the existence of man on earth; they are a human, not a pathological phenomenon. It is only since Freud that we have been able to relate dreams which the dreamers themselves could not understand to their psychic substructure. Can scientific psychology afford any other examples of a psychic phenomenon so common, coeval with humanity itself, incomprehensible for such countless ages, and yet explained at last?

Freud's work is the most profound analysis that history has ever known of the less human elements in human nature.[96]

It could perhaps be put more generously, and I believe that it is fair that it should. Freud himself was a sincere and generous man, as well as a genius. All his life he had looked upon human frailty without revulsion and without contempt. He had struggled to help man find a way to elevate himself above the savage beast, which, through no fault of his own, is always part of him. The doctrine of original sin found no opposition from Freud, although his explanation of it was biological rather than religious. But just as he accepted man as he was, and strove to make him more free, more responsible, and therefore more noble, so Freud would never accept that man's inherent guilt should be a reason for blaming him. Here at least the Godless Jew was at one with perhaps the most epochal of all Converts to Christianity: *Epistle of St. Paul to the Ephesians, Chapter 6, verse 12.*

. . . For our contention is not with the blood and the flesh, but with dominion, with authority, with the blind world rulers of this life, with the spirit of evil in things heavenly. . . .[97]

London – Rhodes –
Dunmore East –
London. 1964.

References as Numbered in Text

The references are given by title first, followed, in the case of those taken from Freud's own writings, by date when first published, and the publication, volume reference and page numbers. As will be seen the vast majority of these references are taken from the Standard Edition of Freud's works, translated by James Strachey in collaboration with Anna Freud assisted by Alix Strachey and Alan Tyson and published by the Hogarth Press and the Institute of Psychoanalysis, London. Since the Standard Edition covers the full extent of Freud's work on psychoanalysis, and many excellent Bibliographies of work by and about him are available elsewhere, no Bibliography is included in the present volume.

All Standard Edition references are abbreviated to S.E. in this list.

1. *If:* Rudyard Kipling
2. *History of the Psychoanalytic Movement.* 1914–16. S.E. Vol. XXV, pp. 21–2
3. *Autobiographical Study.* 1925–6. S.E. Vol. XX, p. 48
4. *New Introductory Lectures and Other Works.* 1932–6. S. E. Vol. XXII, pp. 137–8
5. *History of the Psychoanalytic Movement.* 1914–16. S.E. Vol. XIV, p. 12
6. *Studies on Hysteria.* 1893–5. S.E. Vol. II. Breuer and Freud, pp. 160–1
7. *Studies on Hysteria.* 1893–5. S.E. Vol. II. Breuer and Freud, p. 6
8. *Studies on Hysteria.* 1893–5. S.E. Vol. II. Breuer and Freud, p. 6
9. *Studies on Hysteria.* 1893–5. S.E. Vol. II. Breuer and Freud, p. 20
10. *Studies on Hysteria.* 1893–5. S.E. Vol. II. Breuer and Freud, p. 9
11. *Studies on Hysteria.* 1893–5. S.E. Vol. II. Breuer and Freud, p. 11

12. 'Intimations of Immortality from Recollections of Early Childhood': Wordsworth
13. *Macbeth:* William Shakespeare. Act V, Scene iii
14. *Studies on Hysteria.* 1893–5. S.E. Vol. II, p. 17
15. *Studies on Hysteria.* 1893–5. S.E. Vol. II, pp. 178–9
16. *Studies on Hysteria.* 1893–5. S.E. Vol. II, p. xxvi
17. *Studies on Hysteria.* 1893–5. S.E. Vol. II, p. xxvi
18. Letter to Fliess, 8.11.1895. Quoted in *Studies on Hysteria.* 1893–5. S.E. Vol. II, p. xxvi
19. *Studies on Hysteria.* 1893–5. S.E. Vol. II, p. 257
20. *Studies on Hysteria.* 1893–5. S.E. Vol. II, p. 256
21. *An Autobiographical Study, Inhibitions, Symptoms and Anxiety, Lay Analysis and Other Works.* 1925–6. S.E. Vol XX, pp. 16, 17, 18, 19
22. *Studies on Hysteria.* 1893–5. S.E. Vol. II, pp. 275–6
23. *Studies on Hysteria.* 1893–5. S.E. Vol. II, pp. 295–6
24. *Studies on Hysteria.* 1893–5. S.E. Vol. II, pp. 301–2
25. *Five Lectures on Psychoanalysis.* 1910. S.E. Vol. XI, p. 33
26. *Five Lectures on Psychoanalysis.* 1910. S.E. Vol. XI, pp. 33–7
27. *The Interpretation of Dreams.* 1900. S.E. Vol. IV, p. xxxii
28. *The Interpretation of Dreams.* 1900. S.E. Vol. IV, pp. 146–7
29. *The Interpretation of Dreams.* 1900. S.E. Vol. IV, p. 279
30. *Morbid Fears and Compulsions:* Frink. (Quoted by Roland Dalbiez in *Psychoanalytical Method and the Doctrine of Freud.* 1941. Longmans, Green & Co., Ltd. Vol. I, p. 77)
31. *The Interpretation of Dreams:* Freud. (Quoted by Roland Dalbiez in *Psychoanalytical Method and the Doctrine of Freud.* 1941. Longmans, Green & Co., Ltd. Vol. I, p. 78)
32. *Morbid Fears and Compulsions:* Frink. (Quoted by Roland Dalbiez in *Psychoanalytical Method and the Doctrine of Freud.* 1941. Longmans, Green & Co., Ltd. Vol. I, pp. 78–9)
33. *The Interpretation of Dreams.* 1900. S.E. Vol. IV, p. 312
34. *Introductory Lectures on Psychoanalysis.* 1916–17. S.E. Vol. XV, p. 151
35. *Introductory Lectures on Psychoanalysis.* 1916–17. S.E. Vol. XV, p. 154
36. *Introductory Lectures on Psychoanalysis.* 1916–17. S.E. Vol. XV, p. 158
37. *Introductory Lectures on Psychoanalysis.* 1916–17. S.E. Vol. XV, p. 164
38. *Introductory Lectures on Psychoanalysis.* 1916–17. S.E. Vol. XV, p. 166

39. *Psychoanalytical Method and the Doctrine of Freud.* Roland Dalbiez. 1941. Longmans, Green, & Co., Ltd. Vol. I, p. 52-4
40. *The Interpretation of Dreams.* 1900. S.E. Vol. V, p. 397
41. *The Interpretation of Dreams.* 1900. S.E. Vol. V, p. 396
42. *Introductory Lectures on Psychoanalysis.* 1916-17. S.E. Vol. XV, p. 170
43. *Sixième Promenade. Les Rêveries du Promeneur Solitaire:* Jean-Jacques Rousseau. (Quoted by Roland Dalbiez in *Psychoanalytical Method and the Doctrine of Freud.* 1941. Longmans, Green & Co., Ltd. Vol. I, p. 2)
44. *The Psychopathology of Everyday Life.* (French Edition.) Introduction by Claparède. (Quoted by Roland Dalbiez in *Psychoanalytical Method and the Doctrine of Freud.* 1941. Longmans, Green & Co., Ltd., Vol. I, p. 2)
45. *Introductory Lectures on Psychoanalysis.* 1916-17. S.E. Vol. XV, pp. 77-8
46. *The Psychopathology of Everyday Life.* 1901. S.E. Vol. VI, p. 70
47. *The Psychopathology of Everyday Life.* 1901. S.E. Vol. VI, p. 159
48. *The Psychopathology of Everyday Life.* 1901. S.E. Vol. VI, p. 148 (Footnote on Darwin)
49. *An Outline of Psychoanalysis.* 1939. S.E. Vol. XXIII, pp. 152-4
50. *Introductory Lectures on Psychoanalysis.* 1916-17. S.E. Vol. XV, p. 306
51. *The Interpretation of Dreams.* 1900. S.E. Vol. IV, p. 130
52. *Three Essays on Sexuality.* 1901-5. S.E. Vol. VII, p. 133
53. *Three Essays on Sexuality.* 1901-5. S.E. Vol. VII, pp. 225-9
54. *An Outline of Psychoanalysis.* 1939. S.E. Vol. XXIII, p. 144
55. *An Outline of Psychoanalysis.* 1939. S.E. Vol. XXIII, pp. 144-50
56. *Introductory Lectures on Psychoanalysis.* 1916-17. S.E. Vol. XVI, pp. 396-7
57. *Introductory Lectures on Psychoanalysis.* 1916-17. S.E. Vol. XVI, pp. 258-9
58. *The Ego and the Id.* 1923-5. S.E. Vol. XIX, p. 152
59. *Psychoanalytic Evidence: A Critique Based on Freud's Case of Little Hans:* Joseph Wolpe and Stanley Rachman. (*Journal of Nervous and Mental Disease,* Vol. 130, No. 8. August, 1960, p. 136)
60. *Two Case Histories.* 1909. S.E. Vol. X, pp. 259-60
61. *An Infantile Neurosis and Other Works.* 1917-19. S.E. Vol. XVII, p. 99
62. *As You Like It:* William Shakespeare. Act III, Scene ii

63. *The Future of an Illusion, Civilization and its Discontents.* 1927–31. S.E. Vol. XXI, p. 111
64. *Beyond the Pleasure Principle.* 1920–2. S.E. Vol. XVIII, p. 59
65. *Beyond the Pleasure Principle.* 1920–2. S.E. Vol. XVIII, p. 60
66. *Three Essays on Sexuality.* 1901–5. S.E. Vol. VII, p. 151
67. *The Ego and the Id.* 1923–5. S.E. Vol. XIX, p. 142
68. *The Question of Lay Analysis.* 1925–6. S.E. Vol. XX, p. 212
69. *New Introductory Lectures and Other Works.* 1932–6. S.E. Vol. XXII, pp. 154–5
70. *New Introductory Lectures and Other Works.* 1932–6. S.E. Vol. XXII, p. 133
71. *New Introductory Lectures and Other Works.* 1932–6. S.E. Vol. XXII, p. 134
72. *New Introductory Lectures and Other Works.* 1932–6. S.E. Vol. XXII, p. 134
73. *New Introductory Lectures and Other Works.* 1932–6. S.E. Vol. XXII, p. 135
74. *Five Lectures on Psychoanalysis, Leonardo and Other Works.* 1910. S.E. Vol. XI, p. 136
75. *Introductory Lectures on Psychoanalysis.* 1916–17. S.E. Vol. XVI, p. 374
76. *The Ego and the Id and Other Works.* 1923–5. S.E. Vol. XIX, p. 49
77. *Five Lectures on Psychoanalysis, Leonardo and Other Works.* 1910. S.E. Vol. XI, p. 33
78. *Five Lectures on Psychoanalysis, Leonardo and Other Works.* 1910. S.E. Vol. XI, p. 145
79. *The Origins of Psychoanalysis, 1887–1902.* 1954. Imago Publishing Co., Ltd., p. 234
80. *New Introductory Lectures on Psychoanalysis.* 1932–6. Vol. XXII, p. 234
81. *Freud. A Critical Re-Evaluation of His Theories:* Reuben Fine. 1962. George Allen & Unwin Ltd., p. 37
82. *The Question of Lay Analysis.* 1925–6. S.E. Vol. XX, p. 233
83. *An Autobiographical Study, Inhibitions, Symptoms and Anxiety, Lay Analysis and Other Works.* S.E. Vol. XX, 1925–6, pp. 249–50
84. *Moses and Monotheism, An Outline of Psychoanalysis and Other Works.* 1937–9. S.E. Vol. XXIII, p. 249
85. *Totem and Taboo.* 1913–14. S.E. Vol. XIII, p. 100
86. *Totem and Taboo.* 1913–14. S.E. Vol. XIII, pp. 156–7
87. *Moses and Monotheism, An Outline of Psychoanalysis and Other Works,* 1937–9. S.E. Vol. XXIII, p. 57

88. *Moses and Monotheism, An Outline of Psychoanalysis and Other Works.* 1937–9. S.E. Vol. XXIII, p. 85

89. *Moses and Monotheism, An Outline of Psychoanalysis and Other Works.* 1937–9. S.E. Vol. XXIII, p. 145

90. *Moses and Monotheism, An Outline of Psychoanalysis and Other Works.* 1937–9. S.E. Vol. XXIII, p. 92

91. *Psychoanalytical Method and the Doctrine of Freud,* by Roland Dalbiez. Introduction by E. B. Strauss. 1941. Vol. I. Longmans, Green & Co., Ltd. p.v

92. *An Autobiographical Study.* 1925–6. S.E. Vol. XX, p. 37

93. *Encyclopaedia Britannica.* 13th edition. Vol. XXV. *Larousse Encyclopaedia of Mythology.* 1959. Paul Hamlyn Ltd., p. 207

94. *A Case of Homosexuality in a Woman.* 1920–2. S.E. Vol. XVIII, p. 167

95. *Psychoanalytical Method and the Doctrine of Freud.* Roland Dalbiez. 1941. Longmans, Green & Co., Ltd. Vol. II, p. 316

96. *Psychoanalytical Method and the Doctrine of Freud.* Roland Dalbiez. 1941. Longmans, Green & Co., Ltd., Vol. II, p. 327

97. *The Wild Goose Chase,* Rex Warner. 1937. Title page. (This is an original translation from the Greek by Rex Warner, and differs from either the Authorized or Revised versions of the Bible.)

Glossary

The following definitions, apart from COMPLEX and PSYCHIATRY, are taken from *A Dictionary of Psychology* by James Drever

ABREACTION: Employed by psychoanalysts for the process of releasing a repressed emotion by reliving in imagination the original experience.

AETIOLOGY: Investigation of the causes of a given phenomenon or series of phenomena: medically, the investigation of the cause of a disease or diseases.

AFFECT: In modern usage any kind of feeling or emotion attached to ideas or idea-complexes.
— displacement of, used by psychologists for the attachment of affect, especially in dreams, to an item or object other than that to which it normally belongs.
— fixation of, used of phenomena in development, where interest, in place of normally expanding and changing as development proceeds, remains attached to objects and ways of thought and action more or less characteristic of early phases.

CATHEXIS: Accumulation of mental energy on some particular idea, memory, or line of thought or action (much used in this sense by psychoanalysts).

COMPLEX: A constellation of ideas with a strong emotional overtone; the process whereby a complex becomes buried in the unconscious part of the mind is called repression (see REPRESSION).

Any constellation of ideas which are associated with strong feelings in a person's mind can legitimately be called a complex; in point of fact they are usually memories of real or imaginary experience, together with the conclusions which the subject has reached about them, and the intense feelings which they have produced. They may be helpful or harmful to his subsequent emotional adjustment, and they may on occasion emerge partly or wholly into the preconscious areas of the mind; although it is the object of the repression to prevent this.

CONDENSATION: Term used by Freud, and his followers, for the partial fusion of two or more ideas, occurring particularly in dreams, and producing a characteristic type of distortion, illustrated by such words as 'alcoholidays' for the Christmas holidays.

DISPLACEMENT: General sense, transfer of an object from one place to another. (Psycho-analytical) shifting of affect from one item to another to which it does not really belong, particularly in a dream.

DISSOCIATION: The breaking off of connexions of any kind, in any sort of combination; used in special sense, originally by French school of psycho-pathology, for a functional interruption of associations or connexions in the mind or in the cortex, upon which the revival of memories and systems of ideas depends, as well as the personal control normally exercised over various motor processes, and producing forgettings, hallucinations (negative), anaesthesias, etc., and generally the phenomena produced by Freudian repression.

DREAM WORK: Accepting the views of previous workers that the dream content consists initially of the various sensory impressions received by the sleeper during sleep, together with the worries of the previous day, and exciting experiences, mainly of the recent past, Freud and his followers argue that to this content repressed trends or wishes from the unconscious tend to attach themselves, but, in order to evade the censorship, and prevent the sleeper from waking, so performing the function of the dream, which is to fulfil the wish to sleep, these trends and wishes modify the existing content, so that they may disguise themselves, the modification taking place in the unconscious, and being called by Freud the dream work.

EGO: An individual's experience of himself, or his conception of himself, or the dynamic unity which is the individual; used by psychoanalysts, in an objective and narrower sense, of that part of the person which, as superficial, is in direct touch with external reality, is conscious, and includes, therefore, the representation of reality as given by the senses, and existing in the preconscious as memories, together with those selected impulses and influences from within which have been accepted and are under control.

FIXATION (psychological): The attachment, generally interpreted psychosexually, to an early stage of development, or object at such stage, with difficulty in forming new attachments, developing new interests, or establishing new adaptations.

HYSTERIA. Nervous disorder characterized by dissociation, high susceptibility to auto-suggestion, variety and variability of psychogenic, functional disorders; by psychoanalysts classified as a psychoneurosis, arising from conflict and repression, where the repressed impulses and tendencies are expressing themselves in the various symptoms, etc., which the patient shows, certain characteristic varieties being specially designated anxiety hysteria, conversion hysteria, fixation hysteria.

ID: Employed by Freud to designate the impersonal mass of interacting energies or forces constituting the unconscious in a strict sense, or what might be designated the structural unconscious, behind the processes making up conscious life, as inner determinants of these processes.

LIBIDO: Term, used by psychoanalysts originally, in its usual sense of sexual desire, but later, in the most general sense, of vital impulse or 'energy'.

MATURATION: In general biology, the attainment of maturity, or the completion of growth; in psychology, rather the process of growth and development itself, as contrasted with the learning process.

NEUROSIS: In the old sense, any activity in the nervous system; in present sense, a functional disorder, psychogenic in origin, of the nervous system, rather indefinitely marked off from psychoneurosis; by psychoanalysts regarded as a conflict phenomenon, involving the thwarting of some fundamental instinctive urge (they also speak, however, of actual neurosis, where there seems to be a physical origin).

ONANISM: Producing the sex orgasm by manipulation, or other artificial stimulation of the genital organs.

PSYCHIATRY: That aspect of medicine which is concerned with the mental element in health and sickness, including mental illness and abnormality.

PSYCHOANALYSIS (spelled throughout un-hyphenated for uniformity): A system of psychology, and a method of treatment of mental and nervous disorders, developed by Sigmund Freud, characterized by a dynamic view of all aspects of the mental life, conscious and unconscious, with special emphasis upon the phenomena of the unconscious, and by an elaborate technique of investigation and treatment, based on the employment of continuous free association.

PSYCHOGENESIS. The origin and development of mental phenomena in general, or particular features or peculiarities of mental processes, as manifested in behaviour.

PSYCHOLOGY: As a branch of science psychology has been defined in various ways, according to the particular method of approach adopted or field of study proposed by the individual psychologist, but a comprehensive definition, which would include all varieties, so far as they can be rightly said to represent aspects of the original and historical meaning of the word, would run in some such way as this: the branch of biological science which studies the phenomena of conscious life, in their origin, development, and manifestations, and employing such methods as are available and applicable to the particular field of study or particular problem with which the individual scientist is engaged; the differences between psychologists are generally philosophical, rather than scientific, differences, and in any case are far fewer, and scientifically far less important, than the points of agreement; the generally recognized branches of psychology are: abnormal psychology, animal psychology, child psychology, genetic psychology, industrial psychology and social psychology.

PSYCHONEUROSIS: Term usually employed, though not always consistently, for the group of functional nervous or mental disorders, less serious and less fundamental than psychoses, of which hysteria may be taken as the type.

PSYCHOSIS: Abnormal or pathological mental state, constituting a definite disease entity; term applied at one time generally to any mental state or process as a whole; a deteriorative psychosis is a psychosis showing progressive loss of mental function.

REGRESSION (psychoanalytical): Reverting of the libido to a channel of expression belonging to an earlier phase of development, or the reverting of the individual to interests and forms of behaviour characteristic of an earlier or infantile stage, often as a result of fixation.

REPRESSION: A conception developed initially by Freud and the psychoanalysts which has largely displaced the dissociation of the French psychopathologists, the essential difference from dissociation being that it is dynamic and explanatory and not merely descriptive; applied primarily, with Freud, to a mental process arising from conflict between the pleasure principle and the reality principle, as when impulses and desires are in conflict with enforced standards of conduct; as a result such impulses and desires, with the associated memories and ideal systems, and the painful emotions arising out of the conflict, are actively or automatically thrust out of consciousness into the unconscious, in which, however, they still remain active, determining behaviour and experience, for the most part indirectly, and producing neurotic symptoms of various kinds, as well as determining dreams, both night and day, and underlying many types of deviations from normal behaviour. Rivers has suggested that the term repression should be employed in its ordinary sense of 'actively thrusting out of the mind', and the term suppression employed for the automatic process, to which the term is practically restricted by Freud.

SCREEN MEMORY: A psychoanalytic term for fragmentary memory items from early childhood represented by something trivial in processes of condensation, in the manifest dream content. Sometimes called cover memory.

SEX: A fundamental distinction, relating to reproduction, within a species, dividing it into two divisions, male and female, according as sperm (male) or ova (female) cells are produced. In psychoanalytic theory sex and sexual are widened so as to include phenomena which have no direct bearing on reproduction, on the assumption that the pleasure derived is of the same order, is in fact essentially the same, in the case particularly of the young child, as that associated with sex phenomena in the strict sense; if in such cases sensuous were substituted for sexual, many of their views would be more readily accepted.

SUPER-EGO: Term employed by psychoanalysts to designate a structure in the unconscious built up by early experiences, on the basis mainly of the child's relations to his parents, and functioning as a kind of conscience, criticizing the thoughts and acts of the ego, causing feelings of guilt and anxiety, when the ego gratifies or tends to gratify primitive impulses.

SYNDROME: A complex going together of the various symptoms of a disease; a symptom-complex.

TRANSFERENCE: Term employed by psychoanalysts of

the development of an emotional attitude, positive or negative, love or hate, towards the analyst on the part of the patient or subject; also used generally, of the passing of an affective attitude or colouring from one object or person to another object or person connected by association in the experience of an individual person or animal.

TRAUMA: Any injury, wound, or shock, most frequently physical or structural, but also mental, in the form of an emotional shock, producing a disturbance, more or less enduring, of mental functions.

Index

More about Penguins and Pelicans

Penguinews, which appears every month, contains details of all the new books issued by Penguins as they are published. From time to time it is supplemented by *Penguins in Print*, which is a complete list of all books published by Penguins which are in print. (There are well over four thousand of these.)

A specimen copy of *Penguinews* will be sent to you free on request, and you can become a subscriber for the price of the postage. For a year's issues (including the complete lists) please send 30p if you live in the United Kingdom, or 60p if you live elsewhere. Just write to Dept EP, Penguin Books Ltd, Harmondsworth, Middlesex, enclosing a cheque or postal order, and your name will be added to the mailing list.

Some other books published by Penguins are described on the following pages.

Note: *Penguinews* and *Penguins in Print* are not available in the U.S.A. or Canada

Two Short Accounts of Psycho-Analysis

Sigmund Freud

These two accounts form the best possible introduction to psycho-analysis for the general reader, for whom they were originally prepared.

When Sigmund Freud was invited to lecture in America in 1909 he expounded, for the first time at any length, the results of his work in Vienna over many years. He described in these *Five Lectures on Psycho-Analysis* his abandonment of hypnosis and his adoption, in order to disclose repressed complexes, of 'free association', the interpretation of dreams, and the explanation of apparently haphazard actions and errors. He devoted one lecture to the fundamental subject of sexuality and spoke of the transference in analysis.

When, in 1926, he came to write *The Question of Lay Analysis,* in defence of a non-medical colleague accused of 'quackery', he had greatly developed his theory of the structure of the mind, with its 'ego' and its 'id', and this pamphlet provides a lively and clear description of psycho-analysis and its relation to orthodox medicine.

James Strachey has added a short sketch of Freud's life to this Pelican edition of his standard translation.

Not for sale in the U.S.A.

Psychology

The Science of Mental Life

George A. Miller

An introduction to the history and present-day scope of the whole science of psychology, with biographical essays on Wundt, James, Galton, Pavlov, Freud, and Binet among the many thinkers who have made significant contributions to its advancement.

Not for sale in the U.S.A. or Canada

Another Pelican by David Stafford-Clark

Psychiatry Today

Since 1952, when the first edition was published,
Psychiatry Today has been reprinted eight times
and translated into French, Dutch, Spanish, German,
Italian, and Greek. Since it first appeared some
important new techniques have been developed in
research and in clinical psychiatry; and some
formerly promising methods and ideas have become
obsolete and been abandoned. This edition has
been revised to take account of those changes.
Otherwise, in spirit and in emphasis, it remains as
originally conceived; written, in the author's own
words, to tell 'something of the practical possibilities
of psychiatry, something of the size of the problem
with which it has to deal, something of the spirit in
which the psychiatrist approaches it, and something
of the solid and sensible help which it is his aim and
duty to provide'.

'It would be difficult indeed to find a factual report
on a technical subject which would provide such
good reading for any intelligent layman' – *The Times
Educational Supplement*

Not for sale in the U.S.A.

Freud and the Post-Freudians

J. A. C. Brown

Freud and the Post-Freudians explains the main
concepts of Freudian psychology and goes on to
review the theories of Adler, Jung, Rank, and Stekel.
Later developments in the orthodox Freudian school
are also discussed, as are those of the American Neo-
Freudians and the Post-Freudians in England.

This is the first book published in Britain to bring
together all these psychological and sociological
schools and criticize them, both from the Freudian
standpoint and that of the scientific psychologists.

Also by J. A. C. Brown:
The Social Psychology of Industry
Techniques of Persuasion